HANDBOOK OF MOTORCYCLE SPORT

Handbook of

Richard Hudson-Evans

Motorcycle Sport

Arco Publishing Company Inc   New York

Published by Arco Publishing Company, Inc.
219 Park Avenue South, New York, N.Y. 10003

Printed in Great Britain

Library of Congress Cataloging in Publication Data

Hudson-Evans, Richard.
   Handbook of motorcycle sport.

   1. Motorcycling.   2. Motorcycle racing.   I. Title.
GV1059.5.H8   796.7'5   78–2771
ISBN 0–668–04629–5

Contents

Acknowledgment   7
Introduction   9

1 TRIALS   *13*
  From Club to International
    Six-day Trials   *13*
  Sammy Miller's Tips   *27*

2 ENDUROS   *29*
  Green Lane Riding   *29*
  Enduro Racing   *38*

3 MOTOCROSS   *45*
  Cross-country Racing   *45*
  Pointers from Chris Horsfield   *52*

4 SCHOOLBOY SCRAMBLING   *55*
  Youth Competitions   *55*
  Schoolboy Trials and
    Speed Events   *57*

5 ROAD RACING   *61*
  Circuit Racing   *61*
  Racing Hints by Paul Smart   *71*
  Barry Sheene's Circuit Guides   *74*
  Sidecar Racing   *80*
  Jeff Gawley on Sidecar Racing   *82*
  Production Bike Racing   *83*

**6 SPRINTING AND
DRAG RACING**   *87*

7 GRASS TRACK   *94*
  Dicing on the Turf   *94*
  Guidelines by Tom Leadbitter   *97*

8 SPEEDWAY   *99*
  Stadium Racing   *99*
  Advice from Len Silver   *104*

9 RALLYING   *106*
  Road Rallies   *106*
  The Police Method   *109*

10 MACHINE PREPARATION   *115*
  Bike Maintenance   *115*
  Race Preparation   *120*

11 CLOTHING   *125*

**12 TRANSPORTING
THE MOTORCYCLE**   *131*

List of Addresses   *137*
  Motorcycle Specialists   *137*
  Motorcycling Organizations   *142*

Index   *143*

Acknowledgment

My thanks go to the following for their invaluable advice for the aspiring motorcycle sportsman: Sammy Miller on trials, Chris Horsfield on motocross, Paul Smart on solo circuit and road racing, Jeff Gawley on sidecar racing, Tom Leadbitter on grass tracks, Len Silver on speedway, and Barry Sheene on riding to win. I am grateful to all these experts for allowing me to bend their respective ears and divulge their secrets for success on two wheels.

My gratitude must also go to such late greats as Brian Stonebridge on his angry little Greeves motocross bike and to Bob McIntyre on his classic racing AJS and Norton singles. When I was a young cycle-riding spectator at local scrambles and treks to Silverstone, they – and countless other characters, now legendary – are surely to blame for their positive contributions towards my addiction to motorcycle sports.

My thanks go also to the Editor and the staff of *Motorcycle Mechanics Magazine*, the long-established and largest-selling enthusiast's monthly, for being allowed to raid their photographic bank. I am deeply indebted to the leading speedway photographer, Alf Weedon, for permission to reproduce his excellent speedway photographs, and to Nick Nicholls and Jim Greening for their close-up shots of the champions.

Some folk are turned on by race-horses, others by greyhounds. Then there are those of us who are fortunate enough to be hooked on things mechanical, which is where the sporting motorcycle comes in. The bike is pure machine, as versatile as a horse, as swift as a greyhound – and fortunately financially within the reach of most. My thanks, therefore, are extended to Mr Edward Butler, one of England's great inventors, for thinking of such an ingenious idea in the first place and thus starting off the whole motorcycle scene. His 'Petro-cycle' appeared way back in 1884. One hopes that we will still be riding two-wheelers in 1984!

Introduction

Somehow a motorcycle is far more 'physical' than any of the four-wheeled alternatives in the mechanized transport sphere. It combines all the exhilaration of speedy manoeuvrability with the total versatility of the faithful horse. Whether you are totally involved in competition-racing or simply hooked on riding just for the sake of it, the sheer sensations of controlling a motorcycle – surging up through the gears, cranking over this way and that for the bends, trickling along a ridge with the surrounding countryside rushing past beneath your tyres, threading your way along a desolate, boulder-strewn track, or just bowling along with the wind buffeting against your face – are all rare experiences, to be savoured. For, once sampled, sporting and leisure motorcycling has a habit of becoming an obsessive but nonetheless thoroughly therapeutic pastime.

Escape unlimited – for all; four cylinders of mechanical joy by the world's biggest bike manufacturers – Honda

The motorcycle, of course, has always had its following. The so-called revived popularity of the two-wheeler is nothing new. Indeed, in the days before the First World War, the motorcycle competitor outnumbered the four-wheeled racer or trialist. With the wider availability of cars during the 'sixties, there was a general decline in the impetus of the motorcycle, but in the 'seventies the motorbike has returned with a vengeance. Owing to the colossal increase in the cost of fuel and car purchase prices and the current problems of storing and parking larger vehicles, the motorcycle is now being seen as a more economical and practical alternative for the road-user; as a result, there has undoubtedly been a considerable upsurge in the following of motorcycle sport.

For the participants, the most popular form of powered two-wheeler sport is trials riding, although as far as the spectating public is concerned, speedway has quietly continued to attract very large crowds indeed. As for circuit racing, the gates have frequently exceeded those for car meetings, admission costs usually being very much lower and the actual racing being far less processional. Here the participant is not hidden from view, buried in some fire- and crash-proof cocoon. Here motorized racing still looks difficult!

The clubs

Two-wheeled sport is overseen by the Geneva-based Fédération Internationale Motorcycliste (FIM), which links up other bodies from as far afield as the USA and the USSR. In Great Britain the governing body is the Auto Cycle Union (ACU), 31 Belgrave Square, London SW1X 8QQ; in the USA it is the American Motorcycle Association (AMA), Box 141, Westerville, Ohio 43081.

Like nearly every sport, the occasional breakaway organizing bodies exist, although none of these organizations seems capable of mastering the sort of financial support which is so vital when it comes to organizing events properly.

Each to his own

The different types of sport open to the enthusiast vary enormously, and range from simple rallies held on public roads which are very often merely social gatherings for owners of the same marque of motorcycle, to trials, which are held mainly off the road, and constitute a very reasonably-priced form of motorcycle sport indeed. Circuit racing, sprinting, grass track racing, speedway, schoolboy scrambling and motocross all offer different degrees of involvement and spectator appeal. There are also those who like trail riding down the ever-dwindling number of 'green lanes' – not in any form of organized competition, but simply for fun. Each one of these activities requires a totally different type of motorcycle, and very often different riding skills too.

Levels of experience

A motorcycle competition can either be run by a club for its own members, a 'closed' event, or it may be open to members of several clubs, a 'restricted' event. The 'restricted' event may be restricted to certain specified clubs, from one or several named centres. Unlike motor car sport, none of these club or restricted events requires participants to have a competition licence.

The next grade up the scale of importance and competitiveness is the national

10

event. To enter at this level, a rider requires a national licence, issued by the governing body to those who are proved to have the necessary experience to compete with the higher-calibre riders. As far as circuit racing is concerned, for example, a rider will be expected to have raced at three closed or restricted events, and will require confirmation of his competence by the Clerk of the Course on his application form.

The highest category of competition is the international, open to all competitors who hold international licences issued by the relevant FIM member body. To obtain an international licence the rider must have competed successfully in several lower-status meetings – and achieved some results too. Very often international licences are endorsed so that only a particular size of machine may be ridden.

A champion's machine – Steve Baker's 1976 750cc OW31 Yamaha

1 Trials

From Club to International Six-day Trials

Today's motorcycle trials have come a very long way indeed from the early 'reliability trials', which consisted of a collection of road-going machines pioneer-motoring over a route mainly made up of public roads, with a few really steep hills thrown in. The hill climbs became all-important, and, from them, special 'sections' evolved. Specialized motorcycles designed for trials work have evolved too, as has a marking system that is peculiar to the trials world.

Of all the types of motorcycle sport, one of the main advantages with trials riding is that technique comes before guts. Even luck has little to do with it. You do not even need to be a 'natural talent' on a bike. It is a game that you can teach yourself, in which more sheer technique is required than in any other field, and in which experience on the trials themselves makes up for any amount of theorizing. Dedicated machine preparation is naturally a vital ingredient too.

What goes on

A trial these days consists of several sections, all of which are 'observed' by marshals. The sections themselves are held on private property off the public road, although very often the sections, generally held over loose surfaces, are linked together by short stretches of public road-going. The term 'loose surface' can denote a range of entirely different surface possibilities – from the most glutinous mud imaginable to a track made up entirely of old tree roots; from bottomless water holes to sheer sandy rock faces.

A typical club trial usually takes place straight after an early breakfast on Sunday morning, covers some 35 miles in total distance, and includes up to 60 sections, all of which are 'observed' by a team of marshals. The object of the exercise is to see how far you can negotiate each section and how few penalties you can incur in doing so. Each section is marked with a 'Section Begins' board and your progress is 'observed' from the moment that your front wheel spindle passes the start line until you reach the 'Section Ends' card. This the trials enthusiast tackles in all weathers, in what is mainly a winter-based season – when the ground itself is as difficult for riding as possible.

While you are trying to ride over a section, if you are unfortunate enough to come to a halt, the marshal will award you '5' penalty marks. In fact, every time you take

Steering a dry course. Nigel Birkett and 310 Montesa – a winning combination

13

your feet off the pedals, even for the minutest of steadying dabs, you will be penalized. The actual marking system employed has become more sophisticated in recent years; formerly it consisted of a '1-3-5' set of penalty points: 1 for one steadying dab, 3 for more than one (as long as the bike was kept moving) and 5 for a complete stop. Latterly, a '1-2-3-5' marking procedure has been employed: 1 penalty point for a single prod, 2 for a couple of dabs, 3 for unlimited footwork, and 5 when the rider and bike can go no further. In fact, the maximum penalty is handed out not only when the machine comes to a standstill, but when the rider leaves the designated course, riding outside a section marker – or falls off altogether!

The best score on any section, of course, is gained by riding the whole way without stopping, with both feet firmly on the pedals, for which no penalties are collected; this is called 'cleaning the section'.

Keeping fit
Trials riding may not look physically demanding or particularly energetic, yet the rider needs to be extremely agile and, especially on some of the longer events, very fit indeed. For even though the machines used these days are amazingly light, and compared to a road machine seem almost featherweight, surprisingly trials riding is an extremely physical sport.

Obviously the machine you use needs to be ultra-fit too. Gone are the days when any old motorcycle would do. Today's trials sections are designed by organizers to provide an increasingly difficult challenge to a set of increasingly sophisticated trials motorcycles. Yet fortunately, at least in the trials world, the ordinary rider can purchase, straight over the counter, trials machines that are every inch as developed as the steeds used by the top factory riders.

Once upon a time, when Britain boasted a world-leading motorcycle industry, British bikes like Sammy Miller's Ariel reigned supreme. Not so these days. The market is dominated either by Spanish machines, such as Bultaco, Montesa and Ossa, or by bikes from one of the Japanese giants who, needless to say, have been quick to enter the worldwide trials bike sales race. The majority of riders opt for two-stroke power, although latterly there has been something of a revival for the traditional, torquier and less noisy four-stroke, upon which Honda, the world's largest motorcycle manufacturer, has been concentrating.

Many lay enthusiasts tend to group all off-road bikes together. If the handlebars ride high and the tyres have cross-country treads on them, they think these are the only considerations that matter. However, a trials bike is neither a trail bike (for on/off road touring) nor a motocross racer; there are many differences.

A trials bike's specification is concocted specifically so that it can tackle the observed sections. It has to be light, nimble, powerful – and yet be capable of plentiful torque and traction. Like any thoroughly versatile machine, even the trials bike has to be a compromise. For in an ideal world you need a long frame to climb hills, while to manoeuvre really tight turns a short frame is best. Extremes of steering angle between forks and frame can be highly beneficial – but this depends on what you want to do with the bike. A really big steering angle results in much better handling in muddy conditions, while a smaller, upright angle gives better steering where the going is firm. The trials bike has to cope with extremes of surface and gradient. It also has to have more than useful ground clearance.

The anatomy of a trials bike

The trials bike

The most usual wheel diameters for a trials machine are 18 inches for the front and 21 inches for the back. The tyres used on British events can only be of a type approved by the ACU, there being a maximum permitted tread depth. The tyres are tubed and retained on the rims with flange bolts; a necessary feature, due to the very low tyre pressures that are necessary for trials work – as low as 5 pounds per square inch for rocky sections, and down even further to 3 pounds per square inch when the mud becomes really bad.

To increase the amount of torque on hand, the two-stroke-engined trials bikes, likely to be in the majority for several years to come, have been getting larger. With a two-stroke, the more cc employed, the more torque achieved. However, the rank beginner ought seriously to consider starting on the bottom rung by going for a 125-cc machine, not jumping in at the deep end. It really is much more difficult than it looks.

It also pays to buy a second-hand bike, at least for your first one. To begin with, you will probably find yourself dropping the machine rather frequently. It is obviously preferable to do this with an old bike rather than a new one. The best

Efficient and functional, by Bultaco

16

On a trial, feet up or else . . . you are being 'observed'

No 5
DOWN-UP
HILL

OBSERVED
SECTION
BEGINS

source for second-hand machines is undoubtedly the classified advertisements in the excellent weekly *Motor Cycle News* and *Motor Cycle* journals.

When you are finally confronted with a possible second-hand choice, ignore damage to the paintwork. It does not matter if the seat is torn either. A trials bike is a workhorse. Mechanical condition is far more important than good looks. An instant starter is a good sign. Start the bike up and turn it off – several times, just as you would do on a trial. Are the wheels in line? If not, is is merely a case of adjustment – or is there something more sinister? Look for cracks in the frame, or ones that have been badly brazed up. Ride the bike around a little. Try each gear in turn, and, sharply snapping the throttle shut, see whether it jumps out of any of them.

As a general rule, most of the over-the-counter production trials bikes should not be experimented with as far as moving any of the controls is concerned. A great deal of development work has gone into finalizing the positions of everything and you cannot improve on it by altering the controls. However, if you buy a second-hand machine, it can be a different matter. If this is the case, stand on the footrests, which should hopefully be as near as possible to the rear fork pivots (as an aid to traction), and your hands should fall conveniently onto the handlebar grips. You should not have to stoop at all, nor should your arms be bent.

Unlike road racing or motocross, where constant and rapid gear-changing is essential, for trials work you do not want the gear-lever positioned so that it can be knocked out of gear too easily. The foot lever should not be too near the foot, nor too far away. You will usually need to select only one gear for each particular section. If you are forced to change mid-section, contrary to the general rule, this rarely needs to be hurried. Indeed, snatched gear-changes break vital traction. Most trials bikes have five gears (though up to six are used) and gearing as low as 40/1 is possible.

To the uninitiated, a trials bike seat looks very uncomfortable. Pedal cycles have more adequate saddles. But the trials rider only sits on his seat between sections. When he is being observed, he rides the pegs, so that he can move the bike this way and that – and move his weight forwards and backwards as necessary. To assist his movements, the trials bike's petrol tank is extremely slim.

As no club trial is likely to take the competitor very far away from the bootful of tools in the faithful tender car, there is absolutely no point in trying to take along too many spares and tools on the event itself. Not only will too many things tend to be cumbersome, but there is also the all-important matter of weight. Besides, as even the best riders fall off sometimes, you should be carrying the absolute minimum of things in your pockets to prevent them causing dangerous abrasions.

However, some essential 'first aid' mechanical items are wise, and many trials riders would not be without a spare plug, a plug spanner to do the job, a small adjustable spanner, a tyre pressure gauge, and a spare chain link or two, as well as a couple of split links. Then, if the trial involves travelling very far from your car, a spare tube and the tyre levers to change it over might not go amiss. However, for most trials it is unlikely that you will have to touch the bike at all, as long as the basic maintenance jobs have been carried out at home before you came on the trial.

Practise, practise, practise
Practice is extremely important. You should learn the basic manoeuvres of taking

your bike over and around the usual hazard possibilities on some waste ground, and not wait until you do a trial. Even the back garden will suffice. Ride in and out of a line of old oil cans or plastic buckets. Really get to know how to ride your bike with extreme accuracy.

Watch the noise, however, particularly if you are riding round your back garden. You do not want to antagonize your neighbours, since you can be prosecuted for causing a public disturbance. In any case, there is no need for a modern trials bike to be at all noisy. In trials, a noisy bike proves nothing. Indeed, where a noise meter is applied, infringement will cost you 10 penalty marks – the equivalent of failing two sections. Certainly do not experiment with home-brewed silencers and exhaust systems; use only proprietary trials bike silencers. They may appear rather costly

Stand up to stay upright, on a Cotton

but the development work will have been done properly. They should allow the engine to produce maximum power while keeping the noise down as much as possible.

As hardly any trials sections are run to time – apart from the occasional tie-deciding section – ride in a section only as fast as you need to. Putting up a good time is of no importance. Besides, if you build up too much speed, you may not be able to make a turn when you have to.

It is relatively easy, with a little practice, to blast up a slope and reach the top. But it is a very different matter having to negotiate turns, within markers, when you have to ride up or down an extremely steep slope at the same time. If you have to make a turn going uphill, then you will have to move your body forward, so that

as much weight as possible is pressed down onto the front wheel to give you some steering. And when you are negotiating a turn round a large rock or old tree stump, do not forget to allow for the back half of the machine. You will need to develop the knack of going past the obvious turning point before turning so that you do not cut across the marker or hazard with your back wheel.

If you over-brake with your front brake, the looser the surface, the more likelihood there is of losing control. In really muddy going, the more you brake, the more you will clog up the front forks and mudguard with mud. Again, if you do all your braking with the back brake, you will increase the likelihood of the machine slewing sideways, and so losing traction and control. If you have to go down a very steep hill, hold the bike evenly with both brakes, as long as your descent is straight down the hill. If the section descends the hill across a slope, try to avoid touching either brake, and decelerate instead. This way, both wheels will be turning, and you should still have some steering, the rear wheel thus standing a better chance of staying behind the front one!

'Wheelies' impress no one, unless you are deliberately lifting the front of the bike to ease it over a log. For obviously when the front wheel lifts off, the only control you have left is the throttle. Particularly when hill-climbing, where lots of power is required to clear the slope, hold the handlebars firmly to prevent them slipping round out of your hands. But do not use all your weight to keep the front end down at the expense of the rear wheel lifting off and your losing vital traction.

The hazards

By far the most difficult hazard on any trials course is rocks. They can make you lose traction, prevent you from steering correctly, and can stop you altogether if they become lodged under the crankcase. Certainly never be scared of indulging in a really good footing session, so that at least you can keep moving and avoid the dreaded 5 penalties for coming to a complete stop.

If the course markers allow you to, steer round large rocks with your front wheel. If the section boundaries do not permit this, and the route up the section demands that you have to traverse the rocks, then try to face them as squarely as possible. Once again, the best way to overcome first-night nerves is for you to have done plenty of rehearsals. The best practice for cliff faces is to master riding over one or more old railway sleepers, or a round-sectioned pole set up on piles of bricks – progressively increasing the height off the ground. You should eventually be able to graduate to tackling an oil drum, laid on its side and wedged so that it cannot roll about (although it can become squashed rather quickly).

When going up to and over a really steep hazard, like a log or a pole between two drums, you will instantly realize that it cannot possibly pay to charge the hazard. If you do, like a horse charging a gate, your bike will merely catapult you over the top of the hazard. Do not approach too slowly either, for insufficient speed will rob you of enough vital momentum to lift the front of your bike off the ground so that the front wheel can rotate, thus assisting the bike's progress over the top of the obstacle.

The next phase in crossing the log is to ease the throttle back so that the rear wheel drives the bike forward and into the straddling position. At this point the throttle should be eased right off, the clutch held in, and the machine edged forward

Not too fast – but not too slow, again on a Cotton

21

on its bashplate (a necessary skid fitted to protect the underside of the engine and frame). You must try to keep yourself on top of the log but, at the same time, pass the machine over the log until the front wheel reaches the ground on the other side. If the bike sticks, rock it backwards and forwards gently to free it. When the front wheel has landed on the other side, apply equal pressure to both sides of the handlebars, so that the forks do not whip round and send you headlong onto the ground. As the back wheel freewheels over the log, ease the clutch in, and apply some twist-grip sparingly to drive the rear wheel back to earth again. As with any manoeuvre on a bike, practice makes perfect.

When you have to go down a hill on a section and you need to reduce speed for a hazard ahead, apply the brakes for both wheels, but only up to the point *before* they lock. Ideally, try not to favour either end of the bike with your weight.

Some people like de-clutching when descending. This can be helpful, although forcing the engine to keep turning does at least prevent stalling. If it is extremely rough on the way down, then you should certainly ride the bike all the way down under power – and not in too low a gear either. A high gear is best for rough descents. This may sound strange, but you will find more control is available.

However, if you are going down a slope without brakes, but on the engine, then you should place as much of your own weight as possible to the back to help the rear wheel's traction. Remember, too, that throttled back two-strokes (particularly when they are really hot) can foul up their plugs. So look ahead – to see what happens at the bottom of the hill and clear up any misfiring in good time!

Unlike riding on the road, when you do have to brake on the loose surfaces of a trials section, it nearly always pays to favour the rear brakes. Try to keep your body vertical too. Always keep a firm grip on the bars, even when you are operating the front brake and clutch levers, by using most of your fingers to grip the bars rather than the levers, only introducing more fingers to the respective lever according to the extent of the effort required. This way, you are less likely to have the bars snatched out of your hands.

If things start to go wrong, whatever you do, do not panic. So often one sees the novice rider coming to a complete stop on a section and collecting his 5 penalty points for doing so, but then also losing his head in the biggest possible way – and somehow landing up at the bottom of the hill in a painful heap. If you do come unstuck, hang onto the machinery – your trials bike is far too precious to be thrown away. Besides, it might hurt somebody. It is also certain to cost less in damages – as long as you fall uphill of the bike.

If you come to a stop, keep control. Do not be tempted to keep the engine running, because when you de-clutch to do so, if the slope is really steep, the weight of the machine and the lack of any resistance from the rear wheel will cause a tendency for it to return whence it came. It is far better to stall the engine instead, then carefully lay the bike over towards the uphill (with yourself uphill of the bike) and, with the bike still in gear and the engine stalled, you should have one brake on the bike that is working without your having to put your foot anywhere near the brake pedal.

If a 'wheelie' suddenly occurs, do not be too quick to correct it, because if you over-react and throttle back, the bike will tend to do the opposite of a 'wheelie' and nose dive into the ground instead.

22

Try to 'take off' as little as possible too. 'Low flying' belongs to motocross, not to a club trial. But if you do find yourself airborne, then remember to keep your engine speed relative to the ground speed, so that when the machine finally does come to earth, it neither nose dives into the ground through excessive deceleration nor rears up on its back wheel trying to loop the loop through excessive acceleration.

Glorious mud

Regardless of the weather, no British motorcycle trial is complete without mud. The best advice on how to deal with it is to remember that speed is best, power should come next, while too much caution usually means that you will fail the section.

Up, up but (hopefully) not too far away either

To succeed in trials events, you very quickly need to be able to recognize the different types of mud. For instance, if the wheel tracks of the previous riders who have tried the section before you have disappeared, it usually means that the mud is very deep. If this is the case, you should try to rush your bike across the surface of the mud as quickly as possible. On the other hand, the mud may be mainly clay, in which case traction will not be so difficult – that is, unless the clay clogs up your wheels. In any case, you ought to make a point of clearing any mud away from your forks and frame before you start any section, so that both wheels can turn freely.

It is not necessarily an advantage to be an early number when a muddy section has to be negotiated. Sometimes, later numbers can go through a mud-free section, thanks to the early numbers clearing it all out of the way with their spinning rear wheels. The later number also has the advantage, of course, of being able to observe which route *not* to take!

Beware slippery mud when it covers hard going. If you are confronted with any, go for a high gear and do not wind on too much throttle – or the rear of the bike may all too easily slide out of line and cost you dearly in penalties. If you see hard going beneath the mud, then make for it. Traction will be much better, but watch you do not lose the front wheel on the slippery parts. Also, if you have to negotiate any sand, it can be very helpful to ride in the tramlines of the previous competitors, because you gain traction and positive steering from your tyres running on sand that has already been beaten down.

Crossing large puddles or, worst of all, fast-flowing streams, can be potentially alarming even for the most experienced competitor. The big snag with water, of course, is that it is often very difficult to tell how deep it is. This is where a really comprehensive and probing reconnaissance pays off. You should choose the shallowest route. If it is unavoidably deep, do not rush into it – as if you were trying to cross a sea of thick mud at speed – because you will only cause a miniature tidal wave, most of which will swamp your electrics and carburettor. It is far better to enter the water slowly – but purposefully nonetheless – having selected the correct gear for the watery stretch before you enter the water. Any wave that you create should occur behind you, a stern wave rather than a bow one. And if you feel the rear wheel being slowed up by mud beneath the water, then wind on the power to maintain your momentum. Certainly do not be scared to have one or more foot-dab penalties to keep moving, or to ease some of your weight off a sinking back wheel. You will quickly learn the wisdom of equipping yourself with some really waterproof trials boots.

Finally, remember to clean off as much mud from your bike as you can before you leave the trial. For by the time you have loaded up and transported everything home, the mud will have dried on and will be much more difficult to shift. You will also be less unpopular if you leave most of your clods of muddy earth at the trials venue rather than in the family driveway. To help you in your cleaning tasks, take along in your tow car's boot a large plastic container full of water and a few assorted nylon-bristle household brushes; washing-up or pan-cleaning varieties seem to work fairly well when it comes to cleaning the awkward nooks and crannies of a trials bike. When you do get the bike home, hose it down to clean away the last specks of earth. Having splashed a great deal of water everywhere, you will need to dry the bike off thoroughly before regreasing the chain. Check all the motor's

A master at work, the great Rathmell demonstrates body lean

nuts, bolts, screws and gaskets. Change the oil in the gearbox and primary chain case, and check the chain thoroughly before re-lubricating it afresh.

So you finally have a go

As with any sport, it is advantageous for the complete newcomer to do some spectating first. With trials, some stints as a marshal could pay dividends too. Obviously you will need to join an ACU registered motorcycle club, and this is the best way to find out when and where the trials are being held, as well as how to become a marshal.

Once you decide to break the ice and actually have a go yourself, try to get into the habit of arriving at the venue in plenty of time for unloading the bike, putting on your gear without rushing, and going through the scrutineering and documentation process. This will give you adequate time, too, to collect your route cards, which you will need to navigate yourself between the various sections. Particularly when you are new to the game, it pays to learn the route, so that you are not hunting on the public road for the right direction to the next batch of sections.

Very often, novices carry far too much fuel, and this constitutes unnecessary weight. Work out how long the trial is going to be, and carry enough for your engine's worst possible fuel consumption.

The need to undertake a really thorough reconnaissance on foot cannot be emphasized enough, and this is another reason for arriving early. When you are working out your route through a section, make sure you choose permanent markers to remind you of your turning points. These reminder points are vital. Obviously you should not choose spectators or marshals, for they invariably have the very human habit of moving away between whiles.

Remember, too, that nearly every section will alter considerably as the trial progresses, due to the passage of many sliding tyres and feet. Try to allow for this. You may need to consider altering your line from the one you originally decided on. Obviously the weather can change things too and upset your planned approach to a section. Do not necessarily believe the old hands as to how a section should be treated. They may be indulging in gamesmanship – or may even be wrong! However, it can certainly pay to copy a really expert rider's run over a section – perhaps the best way of all to learn.

On a trial, there is always a fair amount of hanging about. Use such time to advantage. Do not waste it in idle banter. Instead, watch the other competitors in action, check your machine, and keep cleaning that mud away. If you need to park your bike anywhere around the course, do not lay it down on its side, even with the fuel turned off, as this can flood the carburettor, thus making re-starting more difficult; it could also cover the controls with mud. Far better to lean it up against a tree or lodge it upright against a tree stump.

Either before or after your reconnaissance on foot, it is a good idea to spend a few minutes warming up yourself and your bike – without overdoing it, of course – just like an athlete limbering up. If you are a newcomer, always opt for taking a penalty of 5 rather than sticking your neck out beyond the level of your experience. Do not be worried about amassing enormous penalty scores on your first few events. Very often on a trial, you will have to tackle some of the sections twice. Try to find out in advance if this is going to happen, so that you can try to learn more about the section the first time through it, correcting your errors of line and approach to hazards during your second chance.

Always be polite to the observers. They are the ones with the right to award you penalty points, after all, and you never know when you may need their help to extract you from the jaws of some particularly evil bog. They are not only unpaid, but *paying* to make your sport possible.

For the vast majority, the club motorcycle trial is an end in itself. For the truly dedicated and ambitious, the national events offer an immense challenge, while the ultimate is to represent the country in motorcycling's Olympics – the International Six-day Trial. At such world-class heights, the delicate artistry of the observed section is replaced in favour of a series of long and flat-out special tests, where the ISDT rider merely has to race against the clock over all sorts of surfaces (which is why many motocross riders have tended to do so well in recent years). ISDT riding is indeed the ultimate, since it is a combination of trials, motocross, and ordinary road riding with the endurance factor for rider and machine included. But it is held only once a year and only for the very best riders.

Sammy Miller's Tips

Sammy Miller's name has become synonymous with trials riding. For after more than 20 years in the competition saddle and nearly 900 awards on the mantelpiece, this one-time professional road racer from Ulster, who once rode for the German NSU as well as the Italian Mondial and Ducati factory teams on the world championship circuits, has undoubtedly become 'Mr Trials'.

Switching from the race tracks to the trials world, after monopolizing prize-givings with Ariel, it was Miller who was responsible for the pioneering work that has put the Spanish motorcycle industry into their current dominance of the off-road bike market. For after long and faithful service on the four-stroke Ariel, he signed for Spanish Bultaco to develop their two-stroke machine into a world-beater – and since the early 'seventies has been attempting to do the same for the world's largest motorcycle manufacturer, Japanese Honda, by returning to the four-stroke fold once again.

Today, Miller heads his own motorcycle accessory and trials retail and mail order business, based in New Milton, Hampshire, which caters for the off-road sportsman all over the world. As a rider he is still a force to be reckoned with, and so his tips on the six main qualities required by a trials rider are certainly worthy of any hard-working novice's attention.

First – even to take part – you need to be enthusiastic, and you certainly will not be an award-winner unless your enthusiasm for what you are doing is unquestionable.

Next, the successful rider must have dedication. Such is the competitiveness of even the smaller events these days that you need 100 per cent effort – and that means before the trial too.

Training may sound rather boring – but I believe you cannot win without it. For if you are not physically fit, you cannot be mentally fit, and if you are not mentally alert, however naturally strong you are, your riding can all too easily fall to pieces.

I do not smoke, and I am a non-drinker. I will not say that either of these things are absolutely vital; I simply find that I ride better without cigarettes or alcohol. Neither of them can help, certainly. Even if you cut your smoking and drinking right down, how much is a very little?

ISDT, 'The Olympics' of motorcycle sport — infinite variety and challenge

In the winter, I go running and attend training sessions with the local New Milton Football Club. I also have a static exercise bicycle. If the weather is good, practice at actually riding a trials bike is of course the best training of all.

The third attribute you need, certainly to win awards on the more important events, is some natural ability. You either have this or you have not. You can, of course, ride without it, but you are unlikely to win an event. Still, taking part is sufficient reward for the majority of competitors.

It is hard to realize that trials riding calls for faster reactions than circuit racing, but I reckon it does. For even though you are never travelling very fast, instant reactions are needed to counter all the hazards that arise so unexpectedly — such as an unseen rock or tree root that appears suddenly and knocks the front wheel to one side. You need instinctive lightning reactions to deal with the unforeseen.

Fourthly, the ambitious rider requires a great deal of self-conviction to overcome some of the pressures that can arise dramatically on the more difficult events. A rider who finds it easy to win awards on small local events must be able to conquer nerves, stay cool and rise to the occasion. This is why an ambitious rider needs to travel to as many different trials as he can afford rather than merely turning up at local events all the time.

Preparation must be high on the list too. Preparation of the bike, yourself, and all the equipment that you need to take with you on a trial. Pay attention to detail. Your riding clothing can be critical — I always take along three different sets of gear to cater for unexpected weather. I have a really storm-proof set of clothing, a medium-conditions riding suit, and a light-weight suit for a heatwave. If you are hot and sticky, then you cannot possibly be comfortable, and if you are half frozen, then you are obviously at a disadvantage beside the rider who is nice and warm.

Finally, the sixth quality for success in trials riding is really the sixth sense — the ability to be able to foresee trouble before it actually happens, and this requires a great deal of experience. One often hears riders who have come unstuck on a section saying that they had bad luck. There is no such thing as bad luck; such riders make their own bad luck — by falling down on one of the six key attributes.

2 Enduros

Green Lane Riding

Trail riding can encompass anything from simply pottering along a leafy track with all the time in the world to riding fast and furiously over lunar-like terrain with a prescribed destination to reach. It is an undeniable fact that simply messing about with off-road bikes has become the most popular and genuinely participatory form of motorcycle sport. For here, the adventurous rider can enjoy the opportunity to do some old-fashioned exploring on uncharted tracks. Here, one can really escape on one's very own mechanical horse.

In the unhurried and spontaneous form of trail riding, it does not matter when the rider arrives, it is how he rides the trail that makes the whole business worthwhile. The rewards for the trail rider are to be found within the vast network of trails, or 'green lanes' as they are called among the fraternity, throughout the country. It is unfortunate, however, that in recent years the number of green lanes left in existence has sadly declined.

This is a sport which allows you to proceed just as fast or as slowly as you want. Even the type of going can be selected according to how energetic, skilful or brave the rider wants to be. Yet, above all, the trail rider can delight in the knowledge that only he or she can truly discover the kind of countryside that no other vehicled visitor will be able to reach.

Apart from the interest of riding a bike over unfrequented tracks, trail riding is a good way to keep yourself in trim, for it requires a surprising amount of energy from the rider. If you are not fit before starting trail riding, then you most certainly will be before long. It is certainly excellent practice for the more serious type of trial or motocross work too.

In Britain, it was not until the massive range of light-weight two-stroke trail machinery hit the market that this branch of sporting motorcycling took off. For although, when equipped with the right tyres, some of the large capacity four-strokes were occasionally taken green-roading by some of their more enterprising owners, their sheer bulk and lack of nimbleness provided a fairly formidable deterrent for inexperienced riders – however adventurous they may have wanted to be. How different today, when there is hardly a range on the market that does not offer one or more on/off road bikes for the customer. However the level of specification you purchase should depend on how much off-road work you really will be doing in a year.

Enduro power – but it must be with torque

In the long term, the best equipment is a proper trail bike from one of the specialist manufacturers, such as Bultaco, Jawa, Montesa or Ossa. If, however, you only require your bike to take you to and from work via a housing estate or two and for a trip along the high street in heavy traffic, a serious enduro machine is frankly rather a waste of time. You would obviously be much better off with a pseudo off-road bike instead, of which the Japanese and East Europeans make quite a range. Ridden with a little common sense and cautious use of the throttle, even over rough going, some of the showroom trail bikes can cope fairly well. In any case, a perfectly satisfactory trail bike can be purchased for considerably less than a competitive trials or motocross machine.

Where to ride?
Obviously the minor roads are good for trail riding, but the trail rider's meat lies in 'RUPP's – 'Roads Used as Public Pathways' – those tracks, usually likely to be unsurfaced, upon which vehicles are legally permitted to travel. You must of course be extremely careful to differentiate between a RUPP which is open to any user, and a piece of track which actually belongs to an individual, who obviously has exclusive right of way. To be legally able to ride along the latter, you will first need to obtain the owner's permission. If you fail to do so, as far as the law is concerned, you are trespassing.

A fairly obvious danger is that you might stumble across what you think is a useful and interesting 'goer', just waiting to be traversed by your machine, only to find that it has been technically decreed a 'footpath' by the local council. If your discovery is guarded by one of the traditional footpath signs, in white on green, check to see if it states that only walkers may use the track. The other forbidden fruit for the trail rider is the designated bridlepath, however suitable for bike riding it may look. This is legally the province of equestrians and pedestrians only; you and your motorcycle are not included!

It obviously pays to know which tracks are RUPPs, and these you can determine by doing some homework on the relevant Ordnance Survey maps before riding into the totally unknown. RUPPs are indicated on OS maps by red broken lines with small intermittent semi-circles. By spending a little time in advance planning, your route through a piece of territory will not be quite so fraught, and you will avoid the inconvenience of finding yourself trespassing on somebody's private property. The OS map will also tell you everything about the countryside over which you plan to ride; the gradients likely to be encountered can be easily spotted from the contour lines; the likelihood of an impassable bog can be ascertained from whether any streams or rivers appear across your path.

As a general rule, of course, the further you travel into the less populated parts of the countryside (and the more spent on petrol therefore), the better value of RUPP you are likely to find. Yet by diligent exploration of your own local map, as well as keeping your eyes open on your travels, you will find an amazing amount of opportunities offered by odd bits of waste ground which might be only a few minutes away from your home.

What to ride?

Before rushing out to buy the ultimate enduro machine, an ISDT replica or some highly tuned 'desert racer', you must carefully consider exactly how much off-road work you are likely to be doing. If you want the machine to double up as road transport, then you would do much better to buy a model from a local showroom rather than from a competition machine specialist.

Once you have tried trail riding and found that it is to your taste, you can part-exchange your 'pretty' machine for something a shade more functional. Although in trail riding one tends to associate four-strokes with the past, both mighty Honda and Yamaha have been doing much to encourage a four-stroke revival among trail bike buyers. Certainly four-strokes tend to be less fussy than two-strokes. They seem to have a better torque performance. But they nearly always tend to be – and feel – heavier. For most British trails, the last thing a beginner needs is some fussy, highly strung and thinly disguised racing machine.

Choose a machine with known reliability, easy starting (and re-starting!), thoroughly developed waterproofing of the electrics and carburettor air-intake, at least eight inches (or hopefully more) ground clearance, and, above all, one which produces the absolute minimum of noise. Fortunately, in recent years, even the most sporting motorcycle manufacturers have sensibly improved their machines in this last direction.

If you intend to tackle trail riding seriously, ensure your bike has such basic common-sense features as hinged fold-up footrests, a beneath-the-engine 'bash-plate' to keep the countryside at bay from the underside of your frame and engine, and, particularly at the back, a flexibly mounted rear and brake light assembly, which should still stand a chance of working after you have ridden along a track.

Flashing indicator lamps and mirrors stuck out on stalks are admirable for commuting but hopelessly ineffective for off-road work. In a very short time they fail to work – if they have not already shaken loose and detached themselves. Preferably remove them in the workshop rather than when you drop the machine for the first of many times!

When it comes to the choice of tyres, even the most unambitious trail work requires, even in high summer, 'trials tyres'. Conventionally-ribbed road tyres are just not good enough. If you do not go head first when the front breaks away, you stand a very good chance of becoming hopelessly bogged down with a complete absence of traction when you hit the first patch of mud. The 'knobbly'-patterned off-road tyres are even better than the smaller and multiblock-treaded trials tyres. Yet for trail work of a touring nature, trials tyres will do admirably.

Unlike on an ordinary road bike, the front wheel should be larger than the usual diameter of 19 inches; instead, a front wheel of 21 inches in diameter is preferable. Such a wheel will avoid falling into every hollow, and will hopefully skate over most of the surface irregularities. The front tyre should not be too wide or the machine's manoeuvrability will suffer; a front tyre width of between 2.25 inches and 3 inches is to be preferred. On the other hand, the wheel diameter at the rear should be smaller than that of a completely on-roadgoing bike, mainly so that there is sufficient room for the larger section rear tyre that is necessary for off-road work. The most usual diameter rear wheel to be found on trail bikes is one of 18 inches, the tyre section being much wider than that used at the front, namely 4 and 5 inches.

However, remember that the larger the tread blocks you use, the less forgiving will be the performance on ordinary roads. Until you really know your machine – and your tyres – you would be wise to indulge only in moderate angles of lean on the corners.

Be prepared

As your confidence increases, you may possibly want to travel the trails even faster. Yet, as in every branch of the sport, increased speeds cost more money, particularly as far as the definite need for more detailed machine preparation is concerned.

After some initial green lane riding with a roadgoing trail bike, you will realize that certain modifications to your machine will be essential. The exhaust system may not be strong enough, mounted well enough, or even mounted high enough for real cross-country work. The suspension travel may simply be inadequate when it comes to coping with a rough track at speed. And almost certainly stiffer shock absorbers will be needed to replace the standard ones.

A standard bike's power (particularly if it happens to be only a 125 cc machine) may well feel inadequate for serious off-road motoring. The standard gearing will almost certainly need to be lowered so that more use can also be made of the higher gears. Then the standard tin and tyre-hugging mudguards need to be changed for light-weight flexible plastic ones, fitted so that there is plenty of clearance for the extra amount of tyre rubber that will be necessary. For a chance at winning, too, a larger diameter front wheel, narrower section knobbly tyre, and smaller diameter rear wheel with wider section tyre, will be top priorities for those who take the game seriously.

A street legal Laverda Chota for real on-off roadwork

You can start trail riding, even quite seriously, for as little as £150, either by buying second-hand or by not setting your sights too high to start with. However, if you become hooked, there will be little change out of £1,000 for an enduro bike that has been specially built for the job. Yet the difference between it and some cobbled-up road bike will, as one might expect, be as a thoroughbred stallion is to a fairground mule.

Donkey tips for donkey buyers

You can, of course, buy a new machine, but if you are a newcomer to trail riding, you will probably drop your motorcycle quite a few times before you learn how to cope with loose surfaces. So it is far more sensible to start with a second-hand machine.

The first advice for beginners is to concentrate on popular models. Specials are all very well, but cannot really be recommended for the total novice, certainly not until he has plenty of mechanical expertise to call on, and knows exactly where to find the spares. However, once he has had some experience of maintaining a trail machine, and has gathered around him some of the basic workshop equipment, then by all means he can graduate to a specialist enduro machine from one of the competition-orientated manufacturers (or to somebody else's one-off 'Green Lane Special').

Yet, however raw his riding expertise, the newcomer should not be tempted to waste money on an unreliable bike, even if it seems cheap at the time. For he will only have to experience the frustrations of his machine breaking down in the middle of nowhere, having to manhandle it up hill and down dale, up to his waist in mud, to be put off trail riding for life. Although there are always many different-priced alternatives to be found among the 'second-hand' columns in the two leading weekly magazines, the novice needs to make his choice carefully. For only if he can buy from a dealer is he likely to have some guarantee of reliability. The best dealers to visit for trail machinery are the specialist off-road shops.

Whether one buys from an individual or a dealer, it is always useful to discover who was the last owner of the machine. If time permits, try to make contact with him and find out why bike and owner parted company. Certainly never buy unless you have given the bike a trial run. If the salesman will not let you start the engine and ride up and down the gearbox a few times, then go elsewhere; there are plenty of other dealers and plenty of other potential purchases on the market.

As a general rule with a used motorcycle, certainly with a trail bike, if the machinery seems to be in a generally good state, then the chances are that it will have been properly serviced, and so will be worthy of your consideration. Avoid a machine that has rounded off nuts and bolt heads where somebody has used a pair of pliers instead of going to the trouble of finding the correct size of spanner for the job. Kinked or taped up cable outers, frayed cable ends or wired-up split footrest or pedal rubbers are all giveaway signs of a penny-pinching previous owner who has not serviced the machine properly.

If the bike has a four-stroke motor, check the cleanliness of the engine oil. To the conscientious enthusiast, cleanliness is next to godliness. Regular oil and filter changes should be part of the owner's creed. For both two- and four-stroke machines, maintaining air-cleaner efficiency is sacrosanct. Take a look at the air cleaner. If the element is really old and looks as if it has not been changed recently, think what the inside of the engine has had to endure. Certainly if both air cleaner and oil are thoroughly dirty, think again.

If you have made an appointment to view a bike, a good tip is always to arrive early. It really is amazing what you can discover by such a ploy. If the individual or the dealer has not been caught in the middle of hastily servicing the machine to be ready for your scheduled appointment, then you can very often gain a more realistic view of the bike's condition. Also, by arriving early, you can see whether the bike has any problems starting from cold. As when shopping for a second-hand trials bike, you should run the engine until it is really hot, then stop it, try to re-start it, stop it again and continue doing this until you are sure you know how the bike reacts when it gets hot. With a trail bike, good starting, hot or cold, is really the number one priority.

Apart from trouble-free starting, look for a smooth engine beat. Ensure that there are no oil leaks visible, and no signs of fresh seeping from what might be a freshly-wiped engine. Try to ascertain whether the suspension still works. Are the forks straight? Is damping still occurring? What are the wheels like? Are they still approximately true? If the bike really is used, be prepared for a little imbalance when you spin the wheels. However, be suspicious of any obvious signs of damage. Look round the rims for this.

If the frame is covered with mud or grease, take the mud off and wipe the grease away to see just what the frame is like beneath. If there are signs of fresh welding, find out why this was necessary. Take a close look at the footrest mountings in particular. They are usually a very good indicator of the way in which a machine has been used, or abused, by the previous owner.

Do not be deterred because a mass-produced trail bike has had its standard fittings altered. Perhaps the flashing indicators have been removed, the standard 7 in headlamp assembly has been substituted for a diminutive 5 in trials version, or the electric horn has been replaced by a primitive (but trouble-free) entirely functional and rather old-fashioned bulb horn. The bike may well be better for such 'anglo' modifications, because the maxim for real trail work should be 'keep it simple'.

However, if you do not want to risk buying a second-hand machine, and cannot afford the latest prices for the brand new, then it may well be that you could find a bargain in the dusty corners of a dealer's shop in the form of an unused last year's model; the fact that it has gathered dust could mean a discount for you. As always, it pays to know the market. And the best way to know it is to scan the advertisements in the specialist weekly press seriously, so that you are *au fait* with current pricing. As far as maintenance costs are concerned, remember that, although not as time consuming in servicing as an out-and-out competition motorcycle, a trail bike still needs much more maintenance per mile travelled than an ordinary road machine.

Riding the trail

The big difference between trail riding and road riding is the degree of concentration which is required. Of course, the purist will insist that even riding to work you need to concentrate 100 per cent. If this is the case, then the off-road rider needs to attain a superhuman level of concentration all the time. On even the humblest green lane, the surface will never be constant, and it takes a great deal of experience to know exactly what you can and cannot do on any particular surface. So until you have experienced all the different kinds of surface, keep the speed to a minimum. You do not necessarily have to travel fast to master machine control. (In any case, slow accidents are so much more preferable to fast ones!)

You need three things to achieve progress along a trail – balance, steering, and the all-important traction. The first two factors are, of course, fairly basic; the third is far more difficult to master. Violent rear wheelspin, and so loss of forward motion, is the most usual mistake that the novice rider is likely to make. The best way to kill this unwanted wheelspin is not necessarily to reduce the throttle opening

A 'mechanical horse' of your own

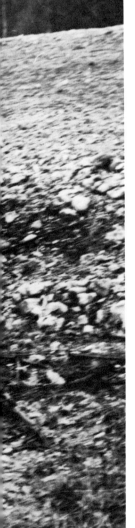

at the twist grip. This will bring an errant rear wheel back into line, it is true, but at the same time could slow you up so much that you could lose all your forward momentum and sink to a stop. Instead, you should try to use as high a gear as possible, changing up and keeping the throttle on – hardly a natural thing to want to do. However, practice makes perfect.

The best way to cope with a piece of rough ground, however slowly you may encounter it, is not to sit down to the job in hand – but stand up! Stand on your footrests, with your knees bent to help absorb any shocks which the suspension may fail to eliminate and which could be transmitted through the bike's frame. For only by standing up will you be able to achieve enough balance to control the bike properly. In fact, for all difficult stretches along the route, you should get up out of that seat.

The other tip is to slow down before hazards. But make sure that you pull through (or over) them under power, not too much power, but certainly with your engine pushing you through. If you are not under power, then you are unlikely to be in control. However, just as in the trials game, if you overdo this cautionary deceleration prior to a hazard, following it up with fierce acceleration over or through the hazard, you will soon discover that there is a constant tendency for your front wheel to ride up high off the ground, as the bike, quite naturally, tries to pivot round its accelerating rear wheel. To counteract this, you will need either to reduce your twist-grip opening or, preferably, transfer some of your weight forward over the handlebars and so over the front wheel, thus preventing it from riding up so easily. In a less extreme way than on a trials section, you can also usefully employ this movement as an aid to clearing obstacles. Certainly the trail rider should realize that body control is almost as important as throttle control.

When slowing or stopping, the golden rule is to use the engine for braking as much as possible rather than the brakes themselves, particularly if the surface is at all slippery. Locked up wheels are all too easy to achieve on loose surfaces and can be disastrous when going down a slope. A sudden locking up of a front wheel, when you are not prepared for it, can very easily tip you off, while if the rear wheel locks up for any length of time, it will quite naturally try to overtake the front wheel.

To go downhill under control, stand up in your footrests, engage a low gear, first or second, and, as the severity of the gradient increases, keep as much of your weight as possible to the rear of the machine. You should use the front brake only if you really need to, and you must always be sure to keep your weight biased towards the rear of the bike.

Obviously, you should try to master the natural fear of using the front brake. It remains the most effective way of reducing speed quickly. Indeed, you should practise locking the front wheel up – on a fairly forgiving piece of territory at first – just to become used to coping with your machine. By easing the pressure off the brake lever to free the locked wheel and putting a leg down pretty rapidly, you will quickly master the necessary business of keeping your motorcycle upright.

When going uphill, the last place you want your weight is too far to the rear of the bike, for obviously you will need to accelerate up a slope and there will be every chance of the front end lifting off and so precipitating a loop-the-loop. So in this case, the reverse applies and you need to place your weight forward.

To begin with, particularly with some of the extremely powerful off-road bikes that are available, spinning the rear wheel can be all too easy. If you do so, you are merely wasting energy, not to mention valuable tyre rubber – and you are losing traction too.

However, correcting rear wheel slides is fairly straightforward. All you need to do is to steer into the slide. If there is not enough room, or time, for the bike's rear wheel to come back into line with the front one, then take some of the throttle off at the twist-grip.

An errant front wheel is another matter altogether. The first thing you need to do is to kill all front-wheel braking. Even over-violent deceleration will tend to push more weight onto the front wheel and can increase your momentum, while obviously too much acceleration is also undesirable, because it will make the front wheel lighter, and so will reduce the likelihood of it gripping. To regain control, an upright bike and a steady throttle are the best cures – as long as you have the time, that is!

Sooner or later in trail riding, you will certainly need to employ your feet. But beware – it is all too easy to jar your leg badly or even break it, unless you are careful. If you allow a leg to trail too far behind you, running over your foot with the back wheel is not impossible either. When footing your way past a hazard or when steadying yourself, keep your knee bent. A jarred straight leg can be very painful. Place your foot as far forward as possible, with the heel down and toes up. Also keep your leg out to one side as much as possible, and as soon as it is back in line with the footrest, return it to the rest.

Practise the basics of machine control as much as possible – but as near to your home as possible too, working on the principle that there will be less distance to push the bike back if you break down. It is surprising how many potential practice places there are in any area, however built up. Take a look around. Use an Ordnance Survey map. For even with the apparent universal scarcity of land, it is virtually certain that there will be, within a relatively short ride from your home, a piece of waste ground that is suitable and legally accessible for practice riding. However, for the sake of the longterm future of the sport, watch your speed and, above all, your noise.

Enduro Racing

When the competition bug bites

The vast majority of trail riders are perfectly happy to do their own thing, pottering along the green lanes in their own time, avoiding being organized. However, sooner or later the competition bug can be picked up by the more enterprising; the call of an 'enduro' may be just too great to ignore. For in its most competitive form, trail riding at speed, not merely against the clock, but against the other riders as well, becomes an enduro, and the devotees rate the challenge of riding largely un-practised and unseen trails as second to none.

The basic concept is to visit a set of predetermined control points within a set of times allowed; failure to stay ahead of the average speeds involves being penalized, so that, at the end of the day, the competitor with the least penalty points incurred is the winner.

Low flying – not for beginners – a Honda trail bike takes to the air

In the United States, however, enduros are really motorcycle races held over a course consisting of various trails, or even across a stretch of desert (and hopefully back again), with all the competitors starting at once.

Whether Stateside or in Britain, enduro riding calls for a very special skill. On British events, the rider is very much on his own, uncluttered by a pack of rivals all around him, as in the case of motocross, or to a lesser extent, at grass-track events. For enduros, machine reliability tends to become more significant, due in the main to the sheer length of the competition mileage, as does the stamina of the rider, especially when an event might involve more than 100 miles of flat-out trail work. Yet perhaps the principal factor has to be sheer experience.

To take trails at any speed, you will need to have mastered the art of lifting up your front wheel so that your bike can be ridden effortlessly over bad bumps. You will certainly be unable to ride swiftly unless you can achieve this necessary manoeuvre just when you want to. Initially, concentrate on perfecting this: power on, move your weight to the back and, at the same time, pull back on the handlebars. Apart from objects that might be in your path, such as old logs, tree roots or rocks, you will need to employ this front wheel hopping to traverse wheel ruts (on a cart track for instance), or to move at undiminished speed onto a higher ledge that may be running parallel to the track that you are on.

Try to avoid too much aerial work. Remember, you will be riding blind on terrain that you are unlikely to know very well, if at all. For when your bike is in the air, it is out of control. Obviously, if you do need to leap uphill or downhill for some reason, then try to keep your excursions from *terra firma* as brief as possible. Remember never to take off while accelerating – and always land with the rear wheel first, not the front.

When leaping uphill, keep your body weight forward, so you do not need to waste time by lifting off the engine's power in an attempt to make the front wheel drop down again. By leaning forward over the bars, you will counteract any desire the bike may have to loop-the-loop. When leaping downhill, keep your weight away from the front wheel and biased very much to the rear of the bike, thus ensuring that you always have a rear wheel landing.

Having to traverse stretches of deep water or, worst of all, mud of unfathomable depth can potentially be the most alarming of the hazards likely to be encountered – and the least pleasant, too. Although you are likely to lose precious time, it often pays to stop and take a good look before you dive in, so that you may determine the best way to make the crossing. The shortest route is not, of course, necessarily the shallowest or the easiest, particularly when it comes to climbing out of a stream.

The model technique for dealing with crossing water is to go into it slowly. Stand back out of your saddle onto the footrests and select a really low gear, so that you can keep your engine turning over very briskly. You will also need to be wary of what is at the bottom of the water, for large rocks and submerged objects may be hidden there – and you need to be prepared for them.

However, do not rush at the water. If you do, you will only risk swamping the engine out with your own tidal wave. Enter the water slowly, but positively, and with plenty of revs on to keep the water at bay from coming back up the exhaust system and stalling the engine. If your ignition system's inspection hatch has been sealed with grease, then the electrics should be able to cope well enough, even if the engine is running several inches below the surface of the water. But if there is a likelihood of water being high enough to interfere with the air filter, then you should turn the engine off before water is inducted, as this can not only make re-starting extremely difficult but has been known to cause serious internal damage to the engine itself.

Much the same advice applies when it comes to traversing muddy tracts. For mud is an even more effective brake than water, and very deep mud entered at speed can almost stop a bike dead. However, if you do trickle into a muddy patch too slowly, you could lose all momentum and stop when you do not want to. The correct way is to enter slowly but deliberately – and under power.

Depth is very often difficult to gauge too. Again, take some time to carry out an inspection if there is any doubt about the extent of the hazard. You should also choose the narrowest stretch to cross, if you can. You want to be particularly wary, having struggled to the other side, that the bank which confronts you is not too steep or awkward to climb. Particular caution is also required for large stretches of unbroken mud where nothing visible appears through the surface which can offer you any grip, for muddy lakes can be deeper than you think.

However, if you do become utterly stuck, do not spin the rear wheel too wildly, as you will only burrow the back of the bike in deeper, thus making it even more difficult to extract. There is no magic formula for rescuing a bike in muddy distress, and even the lightest machine seems to grow heavier the longer you have to heave at it.

You should first try to lift each end out of the mud in turn, hopefully persuading one or other end onto the nearest piece of hard ground. Very often, beneath the mud, there can be some hard earth or rocks which might afford some grip. However, if you do find it absolutely impossible to push the bike either forward or backwards – or even lift either end out of the mud – try rocking the machine sideways out of its wheel tracks and then laying it on its side to spread its weight over a larger area of mud. This descreases the likelihood of the machine sinking too far into the surface. If it simply will not move at all, dismount to reduce the weight above the sunken rear wheel. It may then be possible by engaging first or second gear and releasing the clutch, to push and walk alongside the machine so that it can be driven out of the mud under power.

Never give up, though. Regardless of how impossible rescue may appear, you cannot abandon several hundred pounds' worth of motorcycle in the middle of nowhere. Surprisingly, the seemingly impossible is always possible in the end.

Certainly, as your experience – and nerve – increases, the chances of your being stuck in the mid or sinking beneath the surface of some stream will greatly diminish. In no time at all, you will probably even be able to rocket downhill where previously you could only steel yourself to trickle gingerly from blade to blade of grass. You will find that instant decisions come easily, where previously you had to stop and weigh up the alternatives. You will be able to pick the shortest route, and yet opt for a series of traverses where prudence dictates. Eventually, opening up corners and ridding from apex to apex, as well as using the natural banking of drainage ditches on the inside of corners, will all become second nature to you.

The rules of the game
Enduro events are, as yet, far from commonplace in the UK. Indeed, you will have to hunt them out in the sporting motorcycle calendar and be prepared to travel a fairly long way from your home to the events themselves. When they are held, they are run within the ACU's competition rules. Competitors must be members of ACU-affiliated motorcycle clubs, preferably ones that specialize in catering for trail riders. Also ACU competition licences will be required.

A typical enduro event consists of a one-day competition, riders starting in pairs within various engine capacity classes as well as two main expert and non-expert categories. Bikes always have to be started with the kick starter, without any outside assistance – upon pain of penalty. So an untemperamental and thoroughly reliable engine is obviously fairly important.

The route between the series of control points should be clearly marked with direction arrows, though occasionally, on smaller events, riders will have to find their way on route cards, which is not so satisfactory. The average speed which will be set for the route will vary according to whether the competitor is an expert or otherwise, the timing being set at 25 m.p.h. for the leading category and 20 m.p.h. for the ordinary clubmen.

In addition to the time controls, where lateness will be penalized at the control clock at the rate of 60 points per minute behind schedule time, there will nearly always be one or more flat-out speed tests, held along particularly arduous stretches of forestry track or in the form of straightforward acceleration tests or hill climbs. For these, the timing will be to the nearest second, the fastest competitor being rewarded with zero penalties, the rest having penalties according to the number of seconds that they finish the test behind him.

Throughout the event, any competitor who arrives at control one hour late (or over) is excluded. This may sound an easy enough target; but for mere mortals, it is not. You will also be penalized if you are caught working on your bike during the event with tools other than those you yourself are carrying on board. So, first-aid spares and sufficient tools to effect wayside repairs must be taken along. Always carry tools on the back of the bike and not in any of your riding suit's pockets – just in case you do fall off!

At the end of the day, the event's overall and category winners will be the riders who achieve the lowest scores. The rest of the classified finishers (an achievement in itself on enduro events) gain different grades of medal – gold, silver or bronze – according to the percentage of the total penalties of the overall winner.

In view of the likelihood of having to travel a long distance to take part in enduro events, and the inadvisability of riding to and from the events on your competition machine, you will find it an advantage to travel by van or by car and trailer. Also, by taking along a helper or two you can make the sport very much less demanding at the officially appointed 'service areas'. Having a spare hand or two to assist you with refuelling, lubricating the chain, cleaning your goggles and giving you some vital refreshment is always preferable to struggling on your own. Besides, if the bike fails to make it, there will be more hands and muscles to call on for its retrieval.

If you are travelling to the event's venue with the level of accommodation that four-wheel transport provides, it is a sensible practice to empty your workshop of tools and spares, on the principle of 'just in case . . .'. However, skill is required in deciding what to take along with you on the bike during the event itself. Storage space is obviously going to be at a premium, while tools and spare parts add extra weight, which will sap performance and over-tax both running gear and suspension. Indeed, taking along too much extra equipment could actually decrease your vital reliability factor. Learning what to pack and where to store it can only come from experience, the experience of covering many competition miles. But be thrifty, and keep your load to the absolute minimum. Closely question the need for every item.

The accepted 'basics' that can be regarded as standard equipment for the enduroist include the spanners and keys which will tighten up the kind of components that might work loose during the event, such as the exhaust and the handlebars; the tools for changing the cables; and the correct spanners to effect release of both wheels (in case of a deflated tyre). With a two-stroke motor, a plug spanner and a spare plug are invaluable. A small adjustable spanner, a screwdriver of suitable type and size to fit fuel line clip screws, points and carburettor screws, a pair of pliers and a mole-wrench are all essential, while rolls of wire and self-adhesive tape for binding pieces up in a hurry, a pair of split links for the chain, a spare set of cables (inners fitted to new outers), a length of electrical wire, and that all-important piece of rag are also extremely useful. Pack the tools in a roll and place them under the seat, if possible. If not, then use a tool bag fitted either to the rear of the saddle or on top of the tank. Tool bags are readily available over the counter from most off-road specialists. It is essential to select exactly the right tools, neither too few nor too many, and equally important to try out all the equipment at home before you depart. Practise all the first-aid jobs until you can accomplish them quickly, and ensure that you have a spanner and screwdriver of the right size to meet every eventuality.

Meanwhile, in your support vehicle you should remember to take along clearly marked containers for petrol or petrol and oil mixed (pre-mixed to the correct ratio), separate engine oil if appropriate, gearbox oil, chain lubricant – and plenty of water for cleaning-up operations. Do not forget a large funnel either, to eliminate messy refuelling stops. Spare inner tubes and tyre levers should also be on hand.

You should also pack a spare set of warm, dry clothing, for you will probably need to change after you eventually struggle past the finish – tired, bruised, over time and medal-less, but nonetheless supremely satisfied with your achievement.

*Jumping downhill;
even for the motocross
man, psychologically
the most difficult*

*Cornering a Suzuki
under power, steadied
with proper motocross
boots*

3 Motocross

Cross-country Racing

The next step after trials and green lane riding, in terms of speed and risk, is motocross. Certainly not for the faint-hearted, this highly popular and worldwide pursuit involves racing motorcycles round a cross-country course. As with any form of motorcycle sport, the participant does not need a large garage or, compared to many other types of motor sport, all that much money either. A perfectly adequate motocross machine, together with the necessary spares, clothing and equipment, can be purchased for under £500 (buying wisely and second-hand, of course), while preparation facilities need only consist of a backyard or garden shed.

Evolution

The international motocross event, in which the results are compiled from several legs, evolved from scrambling, which was peculiarly English and consisted of several separate races. Interestingly, the very first cross-country motorcycle competitions were held by the employees of the famous Scott motorcycle factory in Yorkshire; they used to compete against each other in semi-official contests (all using Scott motorcycles, of course) several years before the First World War. This event was the forerunner of the celebrated Scott Trial, which has survived to this day as one of the classic trials on the British calendar; it incorporates both 'observed' and 'timed' sections, and comprises a very special annual challenge over the worst going that the Yorkshire moors can provide.

In the years leading up to the Second World War, motocross riders tended to use what were basically road machines. The four-stroke ruled supreme, with such nostalgic marques as BSA, Matchless, AJS and Norton in the lead. But where are they now? Even during the late 'forties, the four-stroke engined bike continued to win, although more and more two-stroke machines, such as the Cotton, Dot and Greeves, were becoming increasingly popular with the competitors. Indeed, right up to the early 'fifties, British bikes and British riders were recognized internationally. Yet gradually the continental mainland riders took over the lead position, where they have remained ever since, apart from a brief resurgence by Jeff Smith and his BSA in the mid-'sixties.

Over the last 20 years, the two-stroke has been used virtually exclusively; recently, however, due to some extremely skilful development work by Cheney and CCM, several BSA-based four stroke motocross bikes have been emerging onto the scene again. The great two-stroke revolution flourished because the machinery was cheaper to produce and buy than the four-stroke alternatives. Then, after a while, motocross riders no longer had an alternative. Handling became more important in a motocross bike than sheer power. The manufacturers made their bikes lighter and lighter, which meant that the performance potential increased anyway.

The main classes for bikes are up to 250 cc, and below 500 cc. Classes recognized in earlier times, such as the 175 cc and 200 cc, have now drifted into obscurity. Although the 125 cc division has recently been proving increasingly popular on the Continent, the class does not seem to be particularly welcomed by British clubmen or organizers. Needless to say, as in nearly every other form of motorcycle sport, Japanese-made machinery has become the most popular choice, although many enthusiasts show a preference for bikes from Eastern Europe, Scandinavia and Spain.

The machine

If you are a complete beginner, it would certainly be wiser to buy second-hand rather than new. Obviously, while you are learning, there will be the occasional 'incident', so you do not want to be too concerned about scratching any new paintwork or denting a virgin petrol tank. It is also better to buy a machine, even a used one, from a dealer rather than a private owner, since with a dealer you are more likely to be able to secure some redress if the bike breaks down completely. Only if you are an extremely adept mechanic, and really know your motocross bikes, should you consider buying from a private owner.

Certainly avoid rushing into any sale, even from the most reliable dealer, until you have explored the market thoroughly. Take your time. There are plenty of second-hand motocross bikes about. It will also pay to follow form by scanning the results of motocross events in the motorcycle sporting press.

Once you have found a good, sound, reasonably-priced second-hand bike, one that preferably has been sparingly used, secure a test ride to ensure that everything works, and all the gears are there. As with buying trials and trail bikes, try starting the bike again and again, from cold and when hot, to discover if it is a good starter.

Avoid buying an ex-star's machine. In becoming a star rider, he will have extracted every last ounce of performance from the bike. In any case, why is he parting with his successful machine? Because it is more than likely worn out. On the other hand, do not be tempted by a really low price, nor buy a recent ex-novice's bike, for he will have used his to learn and you could very well be paying for his privilege.

Steer clear of an unusual bike, as spares availability may be a problem, and knowhow may be scarce. If you choose a popular type of motocross bike, then bits and pieces will be available in abundance and plenty of people around the motocross scene will know exactly how to carry out every job.

A very good guide to a four-stroke engine's condition is to examine its oil. Take a look at the air filter element too. If they are both really mucky, you will know that the internal mechanical condition could be suspect. Check for oil leaks. Take a look at the sparking plug – has it been changed recently? Has the chain had any attention? Are all three cables bone dry – or have they ever seen any grease? Take a really close look at the frame for cracks. Have any of the welds been patched up recently? Once again, are the footrest mountings sound? Do both wheels run approximately true? Is there any excess play in either wheel bearing? As far as the suspension goes, does it work, both in terms of springing as well as damping?

Providing your detailed examination of the bike passes without too many costly faults arising for attention, then proceed with the purchase. It is wiser in the long run to spend a few more pounds for a bike that has been reasonably well looked after than to try and save a little on one that has not. A motocross bike is not nearly as sophisticated as a circuit racer, but, like any mechanical device, it does need looking after. Fortunately, none of the essential maintenance tasks are very complicated, and a person with no more than average mechanical ability and the normal sort of motorcycle enthusiast's tools should be able to cope without too many problems.

Right from the start of ownership, try to develop the habit of doing all the work to the bike before you leave home for the meeting. The conditions will not only be far more suitable in your own workshop, as opposed to being at the mercy of the weather, dust or mud in the corner of a field, but all your available time at the meeting can be more usefully employed in learning the course and concentrating on the racing.

Skidding and jumping

Motocross riding is not as difficult as it looks, not until you want to ride to win, anyway, but it is different. The relative narrowness and number of hazards on the typical motocross circuit lap call for extreme concentration. You have to be fit too.

The first thing to become apparent to the novice is the relatively high power to weight ratio that applies to even the most average motocross bike. If you open the throttle as you would on a road motorcycle, the amount of rear wheelspin will confirm the fact soon enough. In fact, even on a fairly dry day, the rear wheel will continually tend to slide out of line. To control this, first of all steer into the skid. If this fails, throttle back as well. Very early on in your motocross riding career you should master the fear of skidding. You should be able to play in a rear wheel slide, under power, as and when you need it. You should find that you can perfect this soon enough with practice. Indeed, after a while, only in the rarest circumstances will you have to reduce the throttle at all.

As long as you can keep accelerating towards the next corner, go for as high a gear as possible, to give yourself greater grip at the back wheel. So often, peak revs in each gear can waste valuable time through wheelspin. Most motocross bike engines have adequate torque to accelerate quickly enough even in the low and middle engine speed ranges. Besides, with less wheelspin there is less chance of the rear wheel sliding out of the steered line – another time saver.

Jumps are undoubtedly rather daunting to begin with. When you are jumping on the level, keep some throttle on. Then as the front wheel lifts off the ground, get out of the saddle, stand on the footrests, keeping both legs bent so that they act as shock absorbers when you land. However, still try to keep the main weight of your body biased towards the rear of the machine. This will ensure that the rear of the bike lands first, preferably just a fraction before the front wheel.

You should not overdo the rear wheel landing, however, or you will have so much weight at the back of the machine that you will encourage a loop-the-loop, with the front lifting off on landing and going straight over the top of you – a very painful experience.

For aviating really long jumps, make sure you really hang onto the bars and keep both feet firmly on the footrests – otherwise you will land before the bike. Having kept the throttle open to take off, you will need to throttle back in mid-air to avoid over-revving the engine. Once again, you want to avoid looping the loop on landing. However, you should try to land with some throttle applied, since with no throttle at all the front wheel will tend to be brought down into an over-violent contact with the ground.

Remember, too, that when you are in the air, the steering will be inoperative, so be sure to keep the bars as straight as possible for when you land, or just have a little steering angle on so that the bike, when landing, will go roughly in the direction that you want to go next.

When tackling jumps uphill, obviously you will need much more of your weight forward to counteract any excessive front-wheel lift-off. If you overdo this, however, you will either bite the dust face first or (less painful, but still time wasting) your vital rear wheel traction will be reduced by wheelspin.

Jumping downhill is certainly the most difficult motocross riding manoeuvre of all. It is psychologically the most difficult action. Yet, as the vast majority of competitors tend to 'chicken out' when it comes to riding competitively downhill, a

Muck and bullets shall not stop him. TV Motocross star, Vic Eastwood, never gives in to a bit of mud . . .

brave but scientific competitor can gain quite an advantage on a course with some downhill jumps. Once again, the rear wheel must land first – if at all possible. So you need to keep your weight biased towards the rear wheel when jumping down a slope. Again, watch your steering. You do not want your front wheel to be over to one side when you land.

Once you have cancelled out most of your fear with confidence and experience, you must build up your speed on entering jumps and on coming out of them. As your new-found confidence increases, you should be able to treat each jump as merely a part of an overall lap, vaulting from jump to jump downhill, while accelerating up the gearbox. The star riders will tell you that it is safer to accelerate when you are taking off, even when going steeply downhill. This is why they are 'stars'.

When to stop

Certainly to begin with, the novice rider is unlikely to be going fast enough to want to use the brakes very much. Very often deceleration has the required effect, the engine is, after all, the third brake. If throttling back is not sufficient, there is always the next gear down the box. Four-stroke engined machines, incidentally, are blessed with much better engine braking than two-stroke ones. On a loose surface, a bike's brakes will be at their most efficient – just prior to locking.

Again practise, practise, practise, so that in the heat of battle, you can cut down your braking to the very last moment. And contrary to what some riders say, even though the surface may be quite slippery, you do need to use your front brake. If it was not necessary, then the weight-conscious bike manufacturer would have discarded it.

In fact, if you want to ride quickly, you will need to brake with both brakes, with the main emphasis on the front one – very much in the conventional way. Really learn the feel of your brakes by braking again and again on a piece of waste ground, so that you can tell when they are on the brink of locking up. That is how you want to use them in action. One good tip is not to use all your fingers on the front brake lever; this can be extremely beneficial in helping you to combat panic application of the front brake with the usual subsequent lock-up.

Apart from decelerating the engine, changing down, a combination of the two, and/or conventional braking, the other way to slow down a bike on the loose is to slide the rear wheel out of line. In any case, you will need to develop this ploy when the surface is really loose and the usual retarding methods have little effect.

Braking by going sideways can also be usefully employed to combine braking with cornering. Besides, it is a very effective way to block the path of – and secure the lead over – riders round the outside of whom you have just ridden, while they were engaged in orderly braking and changing down! But be sure to slide the rear of the bike under the controlling influence of power, and not with the panic application of a locked-up rear wheel. Slowing up the bike by throwing it sideways, too, can be mastered – but only with practice.

Using your foot as a third wheel is very much a matter of personal preference, style and circumstance. It can be the quickest way of all to break your leg. On the other hand, it can be the only way to stay in the saddle. Basically, the tighter the line, the flatter the corner or the more adverse the camber, the greater will be the need to employ some steadying footwork on the inside of the corner. However, you must wear proper motocross boots to avoid damaging yourself and to do the job properly. You will certainly be in more control of the situation if you try to develop a style whereby you can keep the upper half of your body as upright as possible, even though the bike may well be laid right over. This is where the steadying foot's combination of vital prop and third wheel comes in. You want to practice 'footing' your way round really tight turns so that the inside leg acts like the point of a compass.

There will be some corners on circuits where the banked effect of the earth on the outside of the turn can be used 'wall of death' style, to greatly speed up corner negotiation. Indeed, the banking can be so helpful that you may be able to avoid using the brakes altogether before the corner.

However, while some ruts can be used to increase your lap times, there are others which need to be treated with the utmost caution. On tramline ruts, for instance, you can all too easily lose your steering and be thrown off your bike before you know what has happened to you. If there is a part of the course where such ruts are travelling in the same direction as you are and you simply cannot avoid them, ride into and along them positively, gripping the bars firmly, yet allowing them to move around in your arms. Then when you can see your moment to escape from the rut, tighten up your arms and steer positively up the side and out of the rut. Do not be afraid to steady yourself with a foot as you do so.

At the meeting

Before you can ride in an event, you will need to have joined a club, either one that is registered with the ACU (the governing body for 'club' events, meetings that are open to centre clubs as well as national-level motocross events in Britain) or the Amateur Motorcycle Association (an amateur association of riders, perhaps strongest in the Midland counties, where sensibly riders are graded 'junior', 'senior' or 'expert' – so there is less chance of inexperienced riders competing in the same races as experts). If you really want to travel round the country or aim to reach the heights in motocross, then opt for an ACU-registered club and one which specializes in organizing motocross. The ACU will provide you with the name and address of a suitable club's secretary.

Having joined a motorcycle club, you should obviously support your own club's events, preferably offering to marshal to begin with. In this way you can learn from first-hand what motocross is all about, and can profit from watching other riders' mistakes.

Scan the weekly sporting press, *Motorcycle News* or *Motorcycle*, for news of forthcoming events, dates and locations, as well as the name and address of each 'secretary of the meeting'. When you write off for regulations, be sure to enclose a stamped addressed envelope. There can be quite a demand for regulations, particularly for the more popular events, and a stamped addressed envelope will not only help the club's funds, but will also ensure that you will receive your entry form at the earliest possible opportunity. Preferably visit a club motocross first, and attend your own centre's events, regularly; in this way, you will get to know your fellow competitors, whose advice can be most helpful, particularly during your vital formative meetings.

You need to be supremely fit for motocross riding, perhaps fitter than for any other branch of the sport. You need also to collect a kit of the right tools so that, if the worst happens, you can tackle jobs at the meetings. I do not advocate doing all your preparation in the paddock, although sometimes things can go wrong even in the best prepared camps. Do not take along the entire contents of your workshop; plan exactly what tools and equipment you will need for each job, and pack the appropriate gear.

Take along some spare fuel; there will not be a petrol pump in the middle of a field. If you have a two-stroke machine, ready-mix your fuel, so that you do not have to do this in the few desperate minutes that may be available between a heat and a final. Pack the right grade of oil for the engine, if a four-stroke. The same advice applies to the primary chaincase, while grease for the cables and an aerosol for the chain should not be forgotten either.

So that you can accurately adjust your tyre pressures, have a tyre pressure gauge on hand, one that actually fits your valves! Take along a sturdy foot pump too. Pick the brains of competitors with similar machinery and tyres – to find out what sort of tyre pressures are being used for the course in question, and for the prevailing weather conditions.

The more motocross events you attend, the more spares you will tend to gather around you. You should certainly retain any parts that you have changed through preventative maintenance, as these can very often be usefully employed for 'first aid' purposes at meetings. You should also take along spare cables for both the brake and clutch levers, as well as the hard-working throttle. Especially for a two-stroke, a spare plug is an essential item, while taking a new chain or at least some new split links and spare links is also a wise precaution.

Do not, of course, forget your own needs. Apart from having a few gallons of water to clean the bike down, you should take along a bucket, a couple of towels, and some soap for yourself. An old bag, in which to put your dirty riding clothes at the end of the day, prevents the inside of the car from being soiled. Keep a spare pair of mud-free driving shoes for the homeward journey; and take along plenty of rags and some de-greasing hand cleaner for cleaning up after you have worked on the bike. Remember too that the refreshment facilities at nearly every event can be fairly primitive. So to keep body and soul happy (a miserable rider cannot ride at his best, after all), be self-sufficient with your catering arrangements. Besides, you will save yourself much money!

You need not concentrate on the route to the same extent as you would for a trials section, but you should still walk the course nonetheless – and preferably twice, too. On the first trek you should become familiar with the lie of the land: which way the corners go, how severe the gradients are and what happens over each brow. On the second round, you should be memorizing the hazards in detail, the locations of any old tree roots that might be poking up through the surface, on which side of the course the best traction can be found, and what is the optimum but practical racing line round the course. It also pays to seek out the short-cuts, if any, to use in the event of another rider's accident blocking your path. These short-cuts might be the only places you can overtake, after all.

When it comes to your turn to practise the course, do not forget to practise the start too. Try to become really familiar with the start, the first dash to the first corner, and the first corner itself. Making a good start, and negotiating the first corner proficiently, are absolutely essential for achieving a clear run in the race itself. Test out the surfaces for traction, too, which is so essential when coming out of the tight corners and for going swiftly up the hills.

Be sure you understand the method of determining the event's results. Will there be a combined result of two legs? If so, you will need to finish each leg. Your cumulative result will be what matters. On the other hand, it may be that your first heat result is all-important, because if you do not do sufficiently well in this you will not qualify for the final.

If qualifying is vital, then pit signals become necessary. These should not be over-complicated – your overall position in the heat is sufficient, coupled with a furious 'wave on' if you are about to be overhauled and ousted from a place in the final. A manageable square of blackboarding is ideal for pit signalling. However, there are occasions when it may actually be to the novice rider's advantage not to qualify for the main final as, by this means, he may then have the opportunity of winning a non-qualifiers' race at the end of the day. So read those regulations thoroughly.

Keep a notebook too, recording any piece of information that could be useful to you subsequently, such as the tyre pressures which were suitable for the course and the weather, and what rear sprocket you used. Ask a friend to time you on a stopwatch; log your practice times and race lap times, as well as those of your rivals. The course may have been changed since the last meeting, but many of the competitors will be the same.

Be content to learn slowly rather than quickly. It is less painful and less expensive. But do try to learn something at every meeting. Pick the brains of the experienced riders. You can be sure that, once upon a time, they did the same. Watch what line the top riders use, and, even if you cannot match their speed, try to copy them.

Pointers from Chris Horsfield

Chris Horsfield has been around the scrambles scene for over 20 years, 16 of them as a professional motocross star. He first raced a converted road bike, a 350 cc BSA B31, and progressed by success from very local beginnings to become a factory rider for James, Matchless, CZ, Greeves, Rickman, Villiers, BSA, and finally CZ again, finishing in the first three for the Czechoslovakian manufacturer in the World Championship in the 'sixties as well as becoming a fireside hero by winning the BBC Grandstand Trophy on TV.

He rates Hawkstone Park in Salop as his personal favourite among all the tracks he has ridden on, with the Farleigh Castle classic, in Wiltshire, as a close second. His most disappointing experience was leading a Grand Prix only to break down with mechanical trouble. His most satisfying victory was when he took the British Experts title at Warwickshire's Larkstone Course way back in 1965.

Today, he no longer rushes all over the world from race to race. For Chris competes in business instead, running his own thriving motorcycle business in Evesham, Worcestershire. The newcomer should heed this former motocross rider's advice, steeped in sheer experience as it is, having been gleaned from worldwide experiences in the saddle.

52

National nostalgia. Chris Horsfield and his 500 cc Matchless doing it for Britain at classic Hawkstone. 1965 lives again

Apart from the mandatory items of riding clothing — such as an ACU-approved shirt, gloves and a helmet — proper padded leather motocross jeans and a body belt (to hold you firmly over the bumps and jumps) are essential. For motocross, you do not need an all-enveloping racing helmet. The helmet needs to be open-faced to allow you to breathe plenty of fresh air (since you do become incredibly hot), and it should be fairly light-weight. In fact, medical experts consider that the amount of exercise expended by a competitor in motocross is matched only by that expended in a top-class game of football: 25 minutes in a motocross race being equivalent to 90 minutes on the football pitch.

It really is very important to be super-fit. If you are not, then you cannot possibly expect to keep up the necessary speed to win. Riding a bike quickly over rough ground taxes every part of you. At the peak of my career, I went for a four-mile run in the morning before going to work, devoted half my lunch hour to physical training and half to swimming, and finished off the day with a four-mile run again in the evening! The easiest and most effective exercises to perform in order to tone up your muscles are press-ups, because they toughen up your stomach muscles as well as your arms and back, all of which come under a great deal of strain on the motocross course.

Do not try to economize when buying a helmet. It is the last thing you should attempt to save money on, so choose a good one — it is your head, after all. Never be tempted, regardless of the conditions, to ride without wearing goggles. Unprotected eyes are so very vulnerable.

Obviously not every competitor wants to get to the top. Taking part is enough fun in itself. However, the top is available to all in motocross, even though it does require the number one attribute — supreme dedication.

If you are successful, it is possible to command £10,000 a month in starts — with prize money on top — in the height of an international season. However, the overheads to be met in order to achieve such a programme and such success are, of course, considerable. There are many more riders — less famous ones — who manage to make a success of being professional, travelling far and wide, and coming out with about £60 profit in a good week.

Motocross is a young man's sport, and the world champions of the future must come from the ranks of the schoolboy scramblers, the best training ground of all.

It is not necessary to be a regular road motorcyclist to be a motocross rider. It certainly helps — but it is not essential. Motocross riding is totally different from riding a motorcycle on the road. When I started in the sport, many people used to ride old road bikes — certainly to learn on. However, such days are well and truly over. For you need a special motocross machine to get anywhere at all these days — and a new one too. Rather surprisingly, most novices seem to buy brand new machines, finding the greater reliability helpful, for the new bike gives much more value in terms of uninterrupted motocross miles.

There is no substitute for experience, though, and the only way to gain this is to enter as many events as you can possibly afford. You should not rush at motocross too wildly, nor should you take risks — the top riders rarely do.

As soon as you arrive at a meeting, you should walk round the track first. This may sound a fairly tedious procedure, but, if you keep your eyes open, it is rarely wasted. In your practice session, spot which lines the more experienced riders use for the various corners and try to copy them . . . rather than keep up with them! And if your race is not the first one, use the time profitably by watching how the leading competitors in this race tackle the course.

4 Schoolboy Scrambling

Youth Competitions

Unlike the four-wheeled side of motor sport (beside karting, of course), it is at least possible for youngsters actually to compete in motorcycling events – and to do so from as young as six years old. Indeed, since its advent in 1964, schoolboy scrambling, the main activity, has positively blossomed into a nationwide craze. Also sand racing, grass track racing and trials events are becoming annually more numerous and, apart from giving a great many young riders some thoroughly worthwhile motorcycle sport, may well pay off one day in terms of producing a pack of world-class adult riders for Britain. In recent years, despite the emergence of Phil Read, Barry Sheene and a handful of trials riders, Britain could certainly have done with them!

Instant schoolboy scrambler

After a few seasons of exploratory piracy, motorcycle sport for youngsters has fortunately come into line and is under the watchful eye of the ACU's system. Youth competitions are now graded in status, in the same way as adult competitions, from 'closed to club' (restricted to members of a specific motorcycle club), and 'restricted' events (where entry is restricted to members of various clubs – but all in an ACU local centre or youth division), to 'national' events (open to members of any club affiliated to the ACU). But unlike adult competitions, a special 'competition licence' is not necessary for any youth competition. However, parents, guardians or a responsible adult must accompany any youth entrant to a meeting – and, what is more, stay for the duration of the time that the youth is competing.

Youth entrants in motocross, sand racing and trials are divided up into four classes according to age: cadets, juniors, intermediates and seniors. The 'cadet' class caters for the six- and seven-year-olds, up to the eighth birthday in fact, with a cubic capacity limit for the engine of 50 cc. The 'juniors' class is for eight- to ten-year-olds, up to the eleventh birthday, with an 80 cc limit for motocross and sand racing and up to 100 cc for trials. The 'intermediate' class is open to eleven- to thirteen-year-olds, up to their fourteenth birthday, with an engine capacity limit of 100 cc for foreign manufactured bikes, up to 150 cc for British ones, for motocross and sand racing events, and a 200 cc limit for trials. The most advanced class of all is for 'seniors', those aged over fourteen up to their seventeenth birthday, with a 125 cc limit if their machinery is foreign made, or up to 200 cc if made in Britain, for both motocross and sand racing, and up to 250 cc for trials events.

Teenage trials bike going down, with rider's weight to rear

For grass track racing, there is one additional class for those in the 'intermediate' and 'senior' age groups, in which intermediates of eleven and twelve years of age (up to their thirteenth birthday), must have machines of only up to 150 cc. Seniors are split at the fifteenth birthday mark, where the limit is 200 cc; up to seventeen there is a 250 cc limit.

In actual fact, after the sixteenth birthday a competitor can compete as an 'adult'. However, once the youngster has mixed it with adult competitors, then there is no going back to clean up in any of the youth division events. When the seventeenth birthday has passed, the young lion has shed cub status and must compete as an adult from there on. If a youngster shows superstar potential and continually wins in his age category, assuming the competitor's parent or guardian (as well as the ACU Young Division Committee) agrees, he can be upgraded into a higher age group.

Such is the popularity of competitive motorcycling for youngsters that over 20 clubs, specifically catering for young competitors, are registered with the ACU, while many adult clubs also have youth sections. Indeed, apart from meetings specifically catering for youngsters, there are very often youth classes included in adult events of 'closed to club' and 'restricted to centre' status.

To help competitors, officials and spectators to identify in which class a young rider is supposed to be competing, the background and number must comply with a colour coding, according to class. The seniors in grass track racing have yellow backgrounds with black numbers; the thirteen- to fourteen-year-old seniors in grass track racing, as well as the fourteen- to seventeen-year-old seniors in moto-cross, sand racing and trials, have blue blackgrounds with white numbers; inter-mediates, whatever the type of sport, have green backgrounds with white numbers; juniors have black backgrounds with white numbers; and cadets have white backgrounds with black numbers.

One thing the complete newcomer must realize from the start is that motor-cycling is entirely different from riding a push-bike – the first few falls will make him realize that. Indeed, being prepared to fall off occasionally is all part of learning not to! Even so, competition motorcycling, particularly before the legal age allowed for riding motorcycles on the road, undoubtedly gives thoroughly worthwhile experience for eventually becoming a very much safer motorcyclist – and motorist, too.

The first thing the interested youngster must do is decide which branch of the sport interests him the most. The best way to find out, without spending too much money, is to become a spectator at as many meetings as possible. If the idea of competing still appeals, then he should go ahead and join a club, preferably a club catering specifically for young competitors. You can find out which one is based nearest to your address by writing to the ACU.

Bikes for young riders
Motorcycles are very much more expensive than even the most sophisticated sports bicycles of course, so you should not aim too high to start with. To see whether you actually like competing yourself, it is prudent to start with a second-hand bike – it is possible to spend well over £600 for a new one.

Once upon a time, the majority of youngsters opted for BSA Bantams, primarily because of their vast second-hand availability. Nowadays, you will find that nearly all the competitors use foreign-manufactured machinery, certainly as far as their engines are concerned.

If you are not concerned with winning for a while, but wish simply to learn the ropes towards the back half of the field, then you can certainly save money by using a second-hand road machine as the basis for your competition steed. However, this quite obviously depends on whether or not you are fortunate enough to have access to workshop facilities.

If you fancy schoolboy scrambling, then a second-hand trials bike very often represents an excellent buy, as it is never likely to have been ridden into the ground. Certainly, apart from those Hondas that are used, the majority of machines in these events are two-stroke powered.

Although realistically it is difficult to purchase a machine that is going to fit a young rider perfectly for several seasons (since the rider is obviously still growing), the frame still needs to fit. To see whether a frame, tank and seat combination fits you, the test is whether or not you can put both feet flat on the ground. If this is not the case, you simply cannot hope to be able to extract the most out of any machine's handling potential without adjustments. Fortunately, it is a fairly easy matter in most cases to make minor adjustments to the height of the seat, simply by removing some of the seat's padding.

Unfortunately, however, running any competition motorcycle does cost money. Although riding prowess counts for a very great deal indeed, far more than is the case in any four-wheeled sporting activity, you do need plenty of money not only to buy a competitive bike but also to maintain it. If the aspiring competition rider is not blessed with an indulgent parent, then he will certainly need to obtain a really lucrative holiday job to pay the bills. Unlike motorcycle sport, sponsorship of any kind is absolutely forbidden, since all riders must retain their amateur status. Schoolboy motorcycle sport is the better for it too.

Schoolboy Trials and Speed Events

Right from the start of a competition riding career, the dreaded rush to events should be avoided. Allow plenty of time to pack up all the necessary kit, and sufficient travelling time to avoid having to break all the speed limits to arrive on time. The only rushing any rider should be doing is when the starter's flag has fallen.

At the event, whether a trial or speed event, avoid wasting time chattering to all the other competitors or trying to impress your own camp followers. It is far better to spend that time walking the course, if at a scramble, or seeing the layout of observed sections on foot, if at a trial.

The penalty system for trials, already described in detail earlier in the book, is perhaps a little strange to the newcomer. The object is to keep your feet up from start to finish of the various observed sections, thus ensuring that your runs are clear of penalties, and so 'clean'. However, if your foot should stray earthwards for even one comforting dab of support, it will cost you a penalty of one minute. Two dabs with the foot, and two minutes penalty are marked against your number by the marshal in charge of the section that defeated you. If you completely fail to cope with an obstacle, and you claw at the ground for support with three or more footfalls, then at least you do not earn yourself any more than three minutes penalty. If you come to a stop completely, ride round the wrong side of a section marker, or miss one altogether, then your error will cost you five minutes worth of penalties. At least with trials, however, the newcomer can compete among fellow novices – that is until an award is won, which will necessitate the young competitor being upgraded to an 'expert' thereafter.

Whether riding in a trial or a scramble, many of the basic loose-surface riding rules apply. It is less painful to stand up in the footrests, accepting the bumps with your own shock-absorbing legs, than it is to let your back take the shocks through your seat. In any case, standing in the footrests actually helps to reduce the centre of gravity, by taking a rider's weight off the bike's seat and distributing it more evenly between both wheels.

In trials, you will not have to encounter many sections before you realize that sheer speed is very secondary to the art of avoiding penalties. Indeed, for virtually any type of event, from a trial to a speed event, starting slowly is essential. Take some time during the inevitable waits before runs to study the lines of the more expert competitors. However, in watching how they cope with the course or sections, be sure to leave yourself plenty of time to transport yourself and the bike to the start line. The last thing you must do is set off in a flustered state.

In motocross, deciding the most advantageous place to position yourself along the start line can really pay dividends. Opt for a first few yards that afford the maximum traction – and that does not necessarily mean searching out the green patches either, there often being more traction from parts of the track where the top grass has been scrubbed off. There is no harm in practising your starts. It can be extremely difficult to overtake on some courses once the race is on.

Leaping like Evel Knievel may look splendid in a photograph and gain a cheer or two from the crowd, but if you do jump the machine into the air every time bumps have to be traversed on an uphill section or along the straight, remember that the driving effect of your engine will have been lost and so you actually risk being slower than the rider who kept his tyres in more useful contact with the ground.

If you have to take off, make sure you do not land on your front wheel first, it being all too easy to trip yourself up. Try to land so that your rear wheel comes down first, just before the front wheel regains the ground and you regain your steering.

One very often sees youngsters 'playing to the gallery' by demonstrating their expertise at mastering 'wheelies'. It may be all very clever, and mighty spectacular, but apart from there being no steering at the time, it encourages 'looping the loop'. The first involuntary loop that I encountered made a horrifying impression on me: the machine shot wildly up into the air and fell back on top of me. Even a light-weight trial bike can do a great deal of damage when it drops out of the sky on top of you, even from no more than a few feet!

Right from the start in riding, try to master the habit of keeping the front wheel well tucked into the corners, thus preventing it from sliding out and the bike being less under control. If a tumble is unavoidable, try to develop the survival habit of covering your helmeted head with your arms. In a scramble event, keep still until you are absolutely sure that the coast is clear for you to reach the sanctuary of the spectator's enclosure before the pack howls round again. When the marshals give you the 'all clear' sign, return to rescue your bike and take it out of the way with you. If you are able (and allowed) to rejoin the action, then it goes without saying that you should be absolutely sure that you do not jeopardize the chances of those who are about to lap you by wobbling back into the race in front of everybody. Wait until there is plenty of room to rejoin the race in relative safety.

Remember to steer clear of any clumps of greenery. Even if there are no solid objects within the foliage, the sudden dragging effect of leaves and branches against the underside of a machine can all too easily cause you to fall. It can very often be much quicker for a rider to choose a course that runs in and out of grassy hummocks, even though this results in taking a line that is technically longer in distance.

While trials riding is excellent training for scrambling – and schoolboy scrambling is a 'must' for eventual graduation to adult motocross – grass track racing, at whatever level, is undoubtedly an excellent training ground for speedway. Grass track events are normally held at courses that are about 350 yards in circuit, with eight riders taking part in each race. In youth motorcycle sport, they are less common than motocross events, though more numerous than sand racing ones which, being held on much longer courses, tend to be very few and far between. Unlike the fairly tight cornering lines that are required by motocross, both grass track and sand racing encourage the intentional drifting that has become the accepted practice of these branches of motorcycle sport.

Really good starts are even more important than they are in motocross, for once somebody has the lead, they can take the shortest possible route – quite an advantage. One thing with sand racing is that, even though it may be the least popular section of the sport in terms of the number of events organized, it is not only the fastest branch of the sport open to youngsters but also the safest.

In speed events, the method of starting can vary. The young rider may be required to start with engine running, in gear, with clutch depressed. The officials may, however, want the engine running but out of gear and in neutral, and just to ensure that nobody jumps the gun, everybody's clutch hands must be touching their helmets.

However, before any youngster imagines that motorcycle sport is merely a matter of being able to ride, I cannot emphasize enough how very important it is to understand the mechanical side of things, too. Becoming a competent motorcycle mechanic really does pay dividends when it comes to riding to win. Besides, a well-maintained bike is obviously much safer than a neglected one.

5 Road Racing

Circuit Racing

Undoubtedly road racing, or circuit racing as is increasingly the case all over the world, is potentially the most dangerous of all the different types of motorcycle sport. The speeds are higher and so are the risks. Even though you may be a fairly competent rider on the public roads, being able to reach from A to B in less time than your friends, riding a motorcycle round a race track, even a circuit made up of closed public roads, is a very different matter indeed. Yet, as befits the risks involved, the rewards for the successful are clearly the highest of all.

Certainly a season or two of avid spectating will not be wasted before any attempt at becoming a competitor is made. Spending an exploratory day or two riding round a racing circuit on an official practice day (both Brands Hatch and Silverstone offer such facilities from time to time) is also a thoroughly useful and formative step to sampling riding on the limit. However, even though a road bike can well be ridden to and at a practice day – and one hopes ridden home again afterwards – it really is extremely rare these days for competitors to ride their machines on the public road to meetings, even when competing in the 'production machine' classes. The sheer competitiveness of all classes of racing, at all levels, has seen to that.

Laverda Jota, about the fastest of the 'Showroom Racers'

As you might imagine, supreme confidence in the preparation of your machine is an essential ingredient. You also need to be physically fit, not to the same extent as a motocross rider, but far more than you might think. It is a disadvantage to be too tall if you intend to ride in the light-weight classes, since crouching down behind the fairing and so cutting down the wind resistance to the absolute minimum will be an obvious difficulty. A heavy-weight rider has a basic handicap too; the smaller the cubic capacity of the engine, the more crucial the all-important power to weight ratio.

Riding bikes on the road certainly provides good experience for circuit racing; for example, the development of an ultra-efficient observation of the road surface ahead is essential, so that oil, wet tar, damp patches in the shadows and loose gravel can be spotted well in time.

In the beginning

The ultimate road test – 24 Hour Endurance Racing

To find out what racing is all about, probably the wisest decision must be to start off with production bike racing. It should help to keep the initial costs down, particularly if, to start with, one of the smaller classes is entered. However, the machine has to comply with the ACU's official definition of what is a 'production bike', as laid out at the end of this chapter. Jumping straight in at the deep end and leaping onto a real racing bike is not nearly so easy as it may look. Certainly, the rider with only fast road riding experience behind him will rarely be able to extract the ultimate from a racing bike.

Greats rub knees. Venezuela's Johnny Cecotto with America's Kenny Roberts. A Yamaha duel at Daytona

Even though on the road scene four-strokes have been moving back and recapturing much of the showroom ground taken by the great Japanese two-stroke revolution, as far as racing machinery goes, particularly in the smaller classes, the two-stroke will be the predominant power-unit choice for many seasons to come. Their maintenance is simpler and so their bills are less.

The exact choice of machine is dependent on the sort of price you are prepared to pay, the range of choice these days being bewildering and the price differential enormous. Until you are truly committed to the racing game, it is probably unwise to consider buying new, there being such a wealth of choice on the second-hand market. You only have to scan the classified advertisements of the weekly enthusiast press to see that. As with other types of motorcycle sport, in terms of having some redress if something were to go wrong with your purchase, it is safer to buy from a dealer, although genuine bargains are now very rare.

One problem when buying a second-hand racing bike is that it is extremely difficult to tell what condition the bike is in unless you can ride it. Taking an unsilenced, untaxed and uninsured racer up the road for a spin is not to be recommended. Even starting it up outside somebody's garden shed on a housing estate is unlikely to be very popular with the neighbours. In any case, firing up a bike and easing open the throttle a few times is hardly a good guide to a machine's mechanical state. So if you can, ask for an internal mechanical check, so you can tell what the expensive part of the bike – the engine – is really like.

Can you select all the gears properly? Do both wheels run true? Have a good look at the tyres to check their overall state, as these have become far from cheap to change these days. Scan the frame for any cracks. Are there any signs that 'the bodger' has been at work? Look for obvious and crude welding repairs. Apply the front brake, at the same time checking for any excessive play in the steering head bearing. What are the springs and dampers like? Do the springs spring, both up and down; and do the dampers damp spring movement and shock?

Then what sort of spares are included in the deal? A spare set of sprockets is essential – but check their condition before you take their existence into account and adjust the price accordingly. Some terrible old bikes have been worth buying in the past simply because of the amount of spare parts that have been included. However, if a test ride is not possible and an internal examination of the engine is not practicable either, then – as a general rule – a sound external condition is usually a fairly reliable sign that the condition of the major part of the bike is likely to be good.

As with other types of racing, it rarely pays to experiment. Unless you really want to be a development engineer, it is nearly always best to race what everybody else does. Once you have decided which type of racing interests you the most, you will need to obtain a 'restricted competition licence' from the ACU, (for a £2 annual charge at the time of writing). This will enable you to compete in 'closed to club' race meetings, as long as you are a member of the particular ACU-registered motorcycle club, as well as 'restricted' events open to members of various clubs in a centre of the ACU. For 'national' meetings, a national grade of competition licence is required, again from the ACU, costing (at the time of writing) £5 a year. Then, when you finally graduate to 'international' events, you will need an international licence, again from the ACU, costing (at the time of writing) £10.

Each year, the ACU publish in their handbook a calendar in which all events run by their registered motorcycle clubs are listed. The clubs and centres are included too, including the names and addresses of the various centre and club secretaries. You should write to organizing clubs' secretaries in plenty of time, asking for the regulations to be sent to you – and do be sure to include a stamped addressed envelope. This will ensure that the regulations are sent to you just as soon as they are published. You will in turn need to send back your completed entry form, together with your entry fee and insurance premium, as soon as you possibly can. These days, there are far more competitors than meetings, and so the demand on the maximum number of entries permitted can be considerable.

Do not be too ambitious in the beginning. Concentrate on the local and minor meetings, preferably ones that clash with larger events on the same day. In this way, you are more likely to be able to get an entry. If your entries are turned down, try to be patient – and keep entering.

Airfield-type circuits are most probably the best ones to start with. They are certainly much safer than proper racing circuits, there being far more room for experimenting with line and maybe running out of road. Besides, airfields teach you to concentrate 100 per cent of the time, as the circuit geography is likely to be less clearly defined than a full-time race track, with its crash barriers, marshal's posts and advertising hoardings. Another point is that you rarely find top riders taking part in the smaller airfield meetings, and so the general speed of things will tend to be slower.

As far as working on your bike is concerned, try to do this at home rather than in the paddock. The facilities offered, even at the so-called top circuits, are nearly always unsuitable as workshop substitutes. Complete the preparations at home – and try to arrive at the meeting with plenty of time in hand. If necessary, consider staying overnight, so that there is absolutely no chance of your arriving late! For most people, budgetary considerations will mean that this has to be camping, either in your bike transporting van, sleeping on reclined car seats, or being under canvas in a tent. Even if funds allow, hotels rarely seem to be able to rise early enough on a Sunday morning to enable you to have the breakfast you will be paying for, before setting off for the circuit in time for the appointed scrutineering session for your class.

You should endeavour to arrive at the scrutineering bay as early as you possibly can, preferably a few minutes in front of your scheduled time, as this will give you the maximum amount of time to be able to rectify any fault that the scrutineer may find. This is particularly important if you have freshly converted a production bike for racing.

The rules demand that 'protective clothing – leather (or approved substitute, which must bear the ACU stamp) in a sound condition, including gloves and boots, must be worn'. The boots must be of leather, and calf length to ensure that the legs are completely covered so that there is no gap between the boots and the riding leather trouser bottoms.

Helmets bearing the ACU stamp, included in their list of approved specifications, in a sound condition and properly fitted, must be worn by all riders for practice and racing. Either open-face or integral helmets may be worn. Goggles, visors or spectacles, if worn, must be of non-splinterable material. (Clothing is discussed in more detail in Chapter 11.) In racing, your riding gear is just as important as your machine, because the scrutineer will check it over at the same time as the bike. You will be expected to arrive at scrutineering ready to race. This will save time having to go back to your tender car or van to find your helmet – and will also ensure that you will be able to practise just as soon as you are allowed to do so.

Race preparation

Try to avoid starting up your engine too far in advance of your practice session, particularly if it is a two-stroke, since when you want to restart it, it may be more difficult. On the other hand, do not leave it until the very last minute before trying to start, just in case it becomes temperamental and causes you to miss your practice session. For if you do not practise, you will not be allowed to race. To begin with, you will need the maximum amount of practice that is allowed for competitors in your class. In addition, it is well worth attending as many weekday practice sessions, which are held at the major circuits from time to time, as your leisure time and finances will allow. Practice on a racing circuit is never wasted.

However, with a four-stroke some warming up is advisable, as you want warm oil to be circulating before you put the engine under any racing stress. It is not really necessary to warm up a two-stroke engine in the same way.

If you find your engine will not start instantly, you must ascertain why. If repeated pushing of the bike and bumping the engine over does not result in the engine starting up fairly promptly, then something is undoubtedly wrong. By continually turning the engine over, you will only increase the risk of flooding the carburettors and fouling the sparking plugs. Also, pushing a bike furiously round the paddock will only over-exert the rider, who should ideally of course be saving all his energies for activities on the track instead.

When a bike does start up properly, avoid the temptation of celebrating the fact by racing up and down the paddock. Not only is this extremely dangerous, but you are hardly likely to make yourself very popular with your fellow competitors.

The two main reasons for practising are, firstly, to check out your bike so that you can discover whether it is going to race properly or not, and whether you have selected the right gearing for the track concerned, and, secondly, to learn all about the circuit at racing speed.

The wisest advice concerning any track, even if you feel you know it fairly well, is to start practising slowly. After all, the track might have been changed since your last meeting: partial resurfacing, a new look to circuit furniture, the removal of familiar landmarks (such as a marshal's post which you may previously have used as a braking point).

You will need to establish your braking, peel off and apex points very quickly. Never use a marshal for these purposes – he might well move between practice and the race!

Try to learn the surface of the track as well as just the corners, looking out for surface irregularities, particularly on the optimum racing line. Talking of line, it can be extremely helpful to see how the top runners tackle each corner. Learn from their practice and certainly do not try to emulate their speed unless your machine is not only as quick but is also blessed with the same suspension, type of tyres and overall standard of roadholding. The right line must come before the right speed, for your lap time is really not all that important to begin with.

Right from the start of your racing career, try to develop a smooth riding style if you can. It is very easy to drift into bad habits, becoming jerky and over-forceful, which not only looks very untidy but does greatly increase the chances of your coming off the bike. Besides, while an erratic-looking rider thrills the crowds, as far as the stopwatch is concerned, he can very often be too slow.

Only when you have gained sufficient confidence in the standard of preparation of your bike, and sufficient experience in riding it on the circuit in question, should you start to worry about extracting the most from your machine's potential. You will quickly learn in the racing game that achieving the most out of any bike is very much governed by the overall gearing that you select for the machine, bearing in mind the circuit being tackled. You can tell whether or not you are pulling the right sprocket on your rear wheel by seeing whether the rev-counter reaches the maximum safe revs permitted for your engine too often. If it does, then you are under-geared. On the other hand, if you find in practice that you are rarely able to pull anything near the maximum permitted rpm for your engine in top gear, you have an over-gearing problem instead. Over-gearing may be preferable to begin with, since there is less chance of over-revving the motor. It will also save a great deal of experimenting if you can find out what sized sprocket some of the other riders, who are using identical machines to your own, are using for a particular circuit.

One other point about learning a circuit, one that is so often forgotten, is that the straights should be given a good pre-inspection too. Due to potholes, filled and unfilled, surface irregularities and so on, some straights can be almost as tricky as corners. You should also research whether there are any potential cross-wind places – due to the lie of the buildings bordering the circuit, advertising hoardings, and so on.

Do not forget your fuel consumption. Try to calculate this as best you can, both from the sort of practice fuel consumption that your bike has been doing as well as the known consumptions of machines similar to your own. Remember that, regardless of the type of bike, more fuel will be used in the heat of a race than will be the case in practice, so err on the side of over-fuelling rather than skimping on it. The weight penalty of carrying slightly more fuel than you need will be very little indeed – especially while you are still learning the ropes.

After practice, you should make a thorough check of your machine. Put the tyres under minute scrutiny. The same goes for the chain; adjust it if necessary. Are all the gaskets holding? Are any oil leaks developing? Take the plug or plugs out, clean and adjust them, and at the same time determine whether the mixture you are employing is the correct one – bearing in mind the rpm being used and the prevailing temperature at the track on the day.

You will need to become familiar with the meanings of all the various flags. As a beginner, there are seven flags with which you need to concern yourself. A red flag indicates 'stop' – just as soon as you can, as the track may be blocked with debris. A black flag with a rider's competition number held up alongside it means that something is mechanically wrong with that competitor's machine; the rider is expected to pull up at the pits before the faulty bike breaks down and endangers other riders. A yellow flag held stationary indicates that there may be danger ahead; if it is waved, the rider should be extremely careful, and be prepared to stop if necessary. A red and yellow striped flag shows that there is oil on the track somewhere, and even when cement has been put down by the marshals to try and mop up the offending substance, you should always try to ride round the oily patch. A white flag means that an ambulance is driving round the track. A green flag shows that everything is back to normal. Finally the chequered flag, held static, means that the race is over, and if it happens to be waved at you, you might just have won!

You should not only learn every corner, but, where there is a sequence of several corners following each other closely, you should also try to perfect the right line for coming out of the last corner at the optimum speed – without falling off! There is little advantage in achieving perfect cornering on two bends only to be defeated by the third. This is undoubtedly one of the most difficult aspects of racing.

The start itself is very important too. Once time has been lost here, so competitive are most races these days, that it is extremely difficult to regain it. As soon as you have mustered onto the start line, stop your engine when you are told to do so; select bottom gear, making absolutely sure that you have done so; rock back the bike onto 'compression', so that the first bump should do the trick when you are finally allowed to start; hold the clutch in and, at the same time, you will most probably find it helpful to keep the bike still by applying the front brake. You should now be ready.

Be sure you know exactly who the starter is, and keep an eye firmly on him. You do not want to be caught unawares. You should have made some time available before your race to see just how he has started previous races. Different starters operate the flag in different ways, so you should know the particular method he is likely to employ.

Do not forget to put your goggles down if you are using a non-integral helmet. They are the last thing you ought to be fumbling with. Make sure you do not forget to turn the petrol and ignition on either – so easily done during butterfly time.

Then, as the flag drops, run forward, ensuring that the bike is moving fast enough before letting the clutch go to turn the engine over, and, at the same time, bump your weight into the saddle. However, make certain you push the machine fast enough for the engine to start cleanly. Like everything else, starts should be practised.

As to what should happen next, there are various schools of thought. Some riders sit side-saddle until they have run out of revs in the first gear, while others prefer to get astride their machines as soon as they possibly can. I think the latter course is to be preferred, as you are more likely to be in control of the machine sooner, and therefore able to manoeuvre it more effectively during the scramble for a good line through the first corner.

Borrowing a tow

Streamlining plays a very important part in racing motorcycling and, even at relatively slow speeds, such as when going away from the start, you should try to tuck yourself in behind your fairing just as soon as you can. During the race itself, you will also need to keep down behind your fairing as much as possible, as flat on the petrol tank as you can, so that you are out of the rushing air: both man and machine therefore being as aerodynamically streamlined as possible.

Straights should be covered as quickly as possible. Work on the principle that the shortest distance between two points is a straight line. Weaving about from one side of the track to the other only increases the distance and so wastes time . . . although, as your experience increases, you may deliberately want to move about the straight to lose a rival from your slipstream. Also, if there are bumps and hummocks on one side of the straight, even though they may well be exactly where the ideal line lies, it can be more advantageous to ride round them – depending on their severity of course.

There is no doubt that slipstreaming can be used to great advantage, and as bikes become faster and faster, so the benefits from slipstreaming will increase too. Not only can you achieve a much higher top speed, tucked in behind a faster competitor, but you can also save your engine too, potentially a most helpful ploy in a long race. For in the slipstream of a similar powered machine, you will be able to pull a considerable number of rpm less than the 'towing' machine by being 'towed' by the air current. Then by pulling out of the slipstream at the very last possible moment – preferably on the approach to the last corner on the last lap – you can gain a most useful bonus in terms of a sudden burst of speed. Correctly timing this break from the slipstreaming tow can allow you to rocket ahead of a rival, from whom you have been having a free and useful tow. The tip here is never to pull out of the tow until the very last moment. If you do, you will only warn the opposition, and thus give him the opportunity to block you off.

However, the dangers with slipstreaming are obvious. To gain the benefit from a high-speed tow, you have to ride really close to your rival's rear wheel, which in itself is always potentially dangerous. Naturally, if you are tucked well down behind your fairing's screen, riding very much in the shadow of the rider and machine in front of you, you will be riding 'blind'. The slipstreaming rider is almost totally dependent on the towing rider not making a mistake. The most worrying moment, of course, is just before each braking point and at the exact (and last!) moment of peeling off to go through a corner. It is therefore safer to break off from the tow just before each braking point, so that you can do your own braking and ride your own line through the corners, planning to regain your tow as you clear each corner's exit and slipstream your way along the straight until you approach the next braking point.

If there is any loose gravel about when you are being towed by somebody, then you will tend to catch the odd loose chippings and, when it is raining, a fair amount of water head-on too. It will obviously be extremely difficult to see anything at all – particularly the vital braking point. So on wet days, especially until you have a great deal of riding experience under your belt, magnetic slipstreaming should perhaps be avoided, or certainly regarded with considerable awe.

The other danger with slipstreaming is that it is all too simple to over-rev your engine in top; this is very easily done, particularly if you are riding in the tow of a much faster machine. This is another good reason for over-gearing, which is often advisable anyway if the circuit has a great many long straights.

You have to slow down sometimes

At the end of every straight there is a corner, and you will have to reduce speed to some extent, according to the severity of the bend. Even your braking point, usually an immovable object, might need to be varied, according to the prevailing weather conditions, by bringing it back up the track in the wet, and so further away from the turn.

The three methods of reducing speed are: sitting up as far as possible out of the fairing to increase the wind resistance – a surprisingly effective windbreak; sitting up and braking at the same time, the main emphasis being on the front brake; sitting up, braking and changing down through the gearbox, to reach the optimum gear not only for the corner but also, most important of all, for leaving it as fast as possible. Remember to complete all your braking before the corner, while the machine is upright and in balance, and while you are sitting fair and square on both its tyres. If a bump upsets the braking and a wheel locks up, you will have more chance of being able to release the brakes momentarily and then try braking again without adding to the drama.

Never try to corner while the engine is on the over-run if you can help it; you should be pushing the bike round under power instead, not to excess, but driving it round – and be under control by so doing. If you do enforce the 'power-on' approach, the rear wheel will tend to slide out of line; this should be corrected as quickly as possible by easing the throttle off, and at the same time reducing the bank of the machine. Whatever you do, avoid slamming the throttle shut too violently, as this will upset the machine's balance even more, and increase the chances of it entering an irredeemable wobble.

Only by achieving the maximum possible speed through the turns will you be able to enter the straights afterwards at the maximum possible speed, and obviously, until you do this, you will not be able to gear the bike correctly; there is always a tendency to under-gear among inexperienced riders.

Ideally, you should straighten out all the bends as much as possible, using all the road width available, for the straighter the line, the less will be the bank of the machine, the more will be the potential grip from the tyres and so the faster will be the potential speed through the corner. However, there will be occasions, due to bumps, potholes or high kerbs lining the inside of the corner, particularly on a closed-public-road circuit, when, surprisingly, the best line (or the safest) will be in the middle or on the outside of the track.

Falling off – and staying on
Sadly, there will be times in racing when you fall off. If it looks as if it is likely to be inevitable, then try to avoid crashing in front of your machine. It is bad enough falling off, without having the machine career into you as well! If things start to get out of shape when you are banked over, the more banked over you are, the less far there is to fall to the ground. Try to slide off behind the machine if you have the choice. After all, it is potentially less disastrous to slide off your bike in a calculated way, rather than go headlong into a wall of fallen riders who may have met with disaster further round the bend ahead of you.

If part of the circuit has a potential jump on it, a rise and fall in the road or a genuine humpback, build up your speed cautiously. And as you go faster and start to take off for longer, remember to keep those bars straight, ease the throttle back slightly when you have lift-off, and try to come down on the rear wheel first. When you are actually in the air, probably the best advice is to do nothing.

It may sound obvious to say that no race is over until it is actually finished, but many a place has been lost in the closing stages of a race. You have only to make a study of the lap times of less experienced riders to see that they tail off towards the end. So to gain an advantage over some of the competition, keep the pressure on the whole way, even if your position does not look too hopeful. After all, somebody in front of you may well be slowing with mechanical trouble, and so their position could be yours as long as you keep going reasonably quickly. When at last you do see the chequered flag, do not be so relieved to see it that you throttle back and sit up out of the fairing too suddenly. Someone could be within inches of your back tyre! Ride on, well past the flag, at an undiminished rate, gradually easing up on the way to the next corner to give the riders following you a chance to ease up in safety.

As a beginner, overtaking other riders will probably not occur very often. But when you do have the opportunity to overtake somebody, do so with caution, and overtake nice and wide. The last thing you want to do is startle and even endanger a slower rider.

Once you are committed to a corner, stick to your line, even if faster riders are about to overtake you. They will have the speed and experience to go round you, but they will not take too kindly to your suddenly altering your line in the middle of a corner. You should be prepared to ride a longer line to keep out of the way of faster competitors.

Pit signals can be helpful of course, but very often they tend to be too difficult for a rider to identify quickly from a sea of pit signallers' boards, too indistinct to read instantly and also too complicated. They should be kept as simple as possible. A rider only requires to know his position or his lap time, the latter preferably giving only the seconds, or a plus or minus sign followed by the seconds according to whether the rider is in front or behind his nearest rival. The main value of a pit signal is to be found on the longer event. There is frankly little time to bother with pit signals on the shorter, sprint-type British club events.

If you are competing in longer events, you will not only want signals from the pits, but you may also need to refuel during the race. If this is the case, practise your pit stops, so that you and your pit crew know exactly who will be doing what when it comes to the race itself. The most usual mistake, apart from the general and time-consuming panic by all concerned, is for the rider to overshoot his pit position. Remember, any time spent in the pit road is totally wasted and very hard to win back out on the track, where an advantage of tenths of a second takes some doing. Also after refuelling, go steady for the first few corners, as the machine's weight will be very different and its handling altered.

Thou Shalt Not

At the time of wiring, the type of racing tyres that a rider may use is restricted by the ACU. This body insists that for any race of national status – or below – only tyres carrying a tread pattern may be used. The smooth 'slick' tyres, the ultimate for dry weather Grand Prix racing of course, are restricted to international riders in international competitions. For 'production machines' only *bona fide* racing tyres with a definable tread pattern, or 'H and V' rated road tyres, are permissible.

The width of handlebars is controlled by the ACU's regulations too. The minimum dimensions cannot be less than 20 inches across. The minimum angle of rotation of the bars, from the centre line turning to each side, must be at least 20 degrees, vital 'stops' naturally having to be fitted to give a minimum clearance of $1\frac{1}{4}$ inches between the ends of the bars on full steering lock and the sides of the petrol tank.

This is so that you do not trap your fingers between the bars and the tank when negotiating a hairpin or when you deftly correct a slide.

The ACU also govern the minimum ground clearance of racing bikes, so that the competitor should be able to incline his bike over to an angle of 50 degrees from the vertical without anything scraping the ground. However, when adjusting your footrests, remember that the ACU insist that they are never fitted higher than 2 inches above the line passing through the centre of the wheels' – with rider and fluids on board. Also, where an oil breather pipe is fitted, the outlet must discharge into an oil catch tank, which must be located in an easily accessible position. The catch tank for the engine oil needs to be at least 500 cc; a gearbox catch tank reservoir 250 cc. Then the engine's oil drain plug must be drilled and wired in position. It is also recommended that non-return valves should be fitted to petrol tank breather pipes; this is likely to be mandatory eventually anyway.

Steamlined fairings are allowed for most classes of racing these days. However, on solos, the full 'dustbin' type of fairing (which used to be used many seasons ago) is not. The regulations insist that the front wheel must still be visible from the sides and any fairing that is fitted must never go forward of an imaginary line drawn through the front wheel spindle. The fairing must not extend back beyond the rear wheel spindle either.

Space for the three necessary competition numbers must be made available, their elliptical backgrounds having to measure a minimum of 9 inches by 11 inches; one number must face forward, and the other two must face to each side of the machine. The figures themselves, either of self-adhesive material or simply painted on, need to be at least 6 inches high and $3\frac{1}{2}$ inches wide, the strokes being at least an inch thick. Their colours vary from cubic capacity class to class: up to 50 cc – white backgrounds with black numbers; 100 cc to 125 cc – white on black; 125 cc to 250 cc – white on green; 250 cc to 350 cc – white on blue; 350 cc to 500 cc – black on yellow; and over 500 cc – black numbers on white backgrounds.

Finally, the maximum permitted noise level that the ACU allow a machine being raced to make is 115 decibels. So, particularly if the bike is 'used', special attention will have to be given to the silencing to ensure conformity and a necessary pass from the noise meter.

Racing Hints by Paul Smart

Paul Smart has been around the motorcycle road and circuit racing scene for long enough to establish his name firmly in the sport's record books as one of Britain's most frequent race winners over the years, as well as having become, after many seasons' campaigning, a respected oracle on every facet of what is really involved in taking part in the race game.

The son of the proprietor of a café which was a regular meeting place for motorcycle enthusiasts, Smart's rise to the top is the stuff that dreams are made of – graduating from spectator to amateur clubman, then rising from the ranks of those taking part to become a work's star for British, Italian, Japanese and American factory teams. And today, even in semi-retirement from full-time racing, Smart has still not forsaken the high-speed world to which he himself has become such a valued contributor. For apart from being married to world champion Barry Sheene's

Paul Smart in his nerveless heyday. His victim for overtaking on the inside 'Super-Frog' Yvon du Hamel for Kawasaki who gives best to Smart's Suzuki

sister, this Kent rider now runs his own Kawasaki dealership in Paddock Wood, from where he still likes to make occasional forays to take part in the events that interest him. Drawing on years of worldwide experience, his advice is therefore highly relevant to the aspiring circuit racer.

I was a regular spectator at whatever events I could get to, from motocross to circuit racing events. I also liked to ride long distances to attend rallies. But after a few speeding tickets, I began to find motorcycling on the road increasingly restricting, so I paid my money and had a go at a racing school at my local circuit, Brands Hatch. The instructor's report stated that I had promise — if I could survive the first few races. . . . Needless to say, this was enough for me. And before very long, I had sold everything I owned to buy my first racing bike — a 125 cc Bultaco.

I cannot recommend strongly enough that a beginner needs to attend a racing school before rushing out onto a track to race. It really is extremely foolish for anybody to attempt to jump in at the deep end without any basic tuition first. Riding on the road — however quickly — and racing on the track are two entirely different worlds.

Perhaps the best advantage in attending a school is that you can find out whether you have any natural ability or not. If you have, all well and good — sponsorship and the chequered flag awaits you. If you find you have not, then this may be the time to pause for thought, and perhaps give up any idea of proceeding further. For racing a motorcycle is not as easy as it seems. Any instructor worth his salt will very quickly be able to spot whether you have any real potential as a race rider or not. If you have not, he will tell you so. If you heed his advice and stick to spectating, you could save yourself a great deal of wasted money. Racing bikes, particularly competitive ones, are becoming increasingly expensive compared with road machines.

I started my racing career in the 125 cc class, which used to be much better supported than it is today. However, I do not recommend that a beginner should buy a larger capacity machine — for while he is learning what racing is all about, the chances are that he will fall off sometimes, and the slower his speed, the less likely he will be to get hurt!

With the demise of the 125s, the best advice for the beginner is to enter the 250 cc production machine class instead. You can start off by using a genuine road bike as your basis – and these days a 250 is quick enough anyway. The next thing is to race at as many circuits as you can, to increase your experience, and race as often as you can afford to. There is no substitute for experience – the more racing the better.

Change from your production machine to a proper racing bike just as soon as you can, certainly for your second season. Always try to buy the best specification that your funds will allow. You should never start a race with a power disadvantage if you can possibly avoid it.

As far as clothing is concerned, never skimp on this. It really is in your own interest, after all. Choose the very best crash helmet that money can buy. I always favour a glass-fibre rather than a plastic one. Wear only real leathers – and only the best. Make sure they fit properly too, for the last thing you should suffer is cramp due to over-tight clothing.

Although you can get away with not being a mechanic – Mike Hailwood did pretty well, after all – it is certainly both cheaper and safer if you really know every nut and bolt of your machine. For only by having intimate knowledge of the engine are you likely to understand just how much you can push it before something will break. Besides, you are more likely to be able to spot the early warning signs that something is starting to go wrong. This could be absolutely crucial – particularly if it happens to be a brake component that is starting to come adrift!

Right from the start of your racing career, you must get into the habit of checking and double checking every nut and bolt of your machine. Do this not only after every race but after each practice session too. This checking became even more vital with the advent of hydraulic brakes; while they are much more efficient, there is more to go wrong. For there are not only caliper bolts, which can work loose, but also hydraulic hoses which can chafe through. Indeed, this was just how I had my most diabolical accident, an incident which effectively put me out of full-time racing. For a brake pipe gradually wore through unchecked, and suddenly resulted in total brake failure!

Never economize on your tyres. After all, they are your only contact with the ground. If their condition is at all doubtful, renew them. You must ask yourself whether there is sufficient tread left to last the race distance – and comfortably. And what happens if it suddenly starts to rain? Always heed the tyre manufacturers' recommendations. They are the experts – and they have tested their tyres in all conditions.

If there is any likelihood of a nut or bolt working loose in a race, particularly if it could cause an accident, always drill and wire it up. Do not be mean with extra clips to secure the exhaust pipe and megaphones – for many races have been lost through exhaust pipes coming adrift and engines losing power in the middle of an event. Rivet the chain, so that it is continuous. Never use the spring split-link that is fitted to road bikes.

If you know somebody who is already in racing, you can cut several corners and find out what is involved simply by helping him out for a few meetings. For by becoming involved behind the scenes in getting a racing bike to the starting line, you will quickly learn that motorcycle racing is not nearly as glamorous as you may have thought it was from reading the magazines!

Contrary to popular belief, only about half a dozen riders in the world are in fact in the superstar earnings league – and as few as 20 or so riders in Britain can truly be said to be wholly professional. Even though a 'name' rider can earn from £500 to £1,500 per meeting in starting money, with prize money on top (if he is fortunate enough to win), he will first need two or three machines of different sizes to be in a position to enter the events. Over a season, the running expenses of funding this sort of operation are considerable.

On the European mainland, it is possible – with luck, and no big accidents or engine blow-ups – to pay your way for a season as a professional road racer. A competent rider who can put up a reliable finishing performance can expect to pick up between £100 and £150 starting money per ride. But this will only really be enough to meet your travelling and running expenses. You will need to be fully equipped with bikes, spares and a reliable van, before you depart for your European summer. You will also need to have established an award-winning record in events at British circuits first.

You must be prepared for accidents too, because sooner or later they will happen. If you see yourself heading for one, and you have the time to think about it – which is unusual – try to get clear of the bike before the crunch comes. This is particularly wise where there is an Armco barrier ahead, for the last thing you want is to be tangled up with the bike when it hits anything. It is painful enough hitting anything on your own! Remember that repairing a motorcycle, however badly bent, only requires new parts, while repairing your body is a different matter altogether. So on the way to the top, do not get into the habit of taking risks. Only when you are at the top are they justified. Indeed, if you are going to beat riders like Sheene, small steps into the unknown are necessary. But such risks always have to be calculated ones.

Finally, do not ignore the requirement of physical fitness. Being super-fit, even for sitting on a racing motorcycle on a flat circuit, actually matters a great deal. For if you have been out drinking the night before, in these professional days, you will be incredibly lucky to win even the smallest club race. Everybody else wants to win too, remember.

Barry Sheene's Circuit Guides

Barry Sheene has been the motorcycle master of his time, in the same way that Geoff Duke, John Surtees, Mike Hailwood, Giacomo Agostini and Phil Read ruled the racing roost before him.

The world championship trail involves mastery of a set of the most testing tarmac ribbons that man can devise to sort out the best of the mechanical wizardry from the might of the Japanese and European motorcycle industry, not to mention the men – like Sheene – from the boys.

Circuit Paul Ricard, France

One of the most recent additions to the circuit circus is in the south of France at the Circuit Paul Ricard, not a converted set of public roads but a custom-built race track, where the most modern safety features exist. Naturally, its designers have incorporated a very varied mix of turns to test rider and machine; corners and straights with radii and length that are also found on many other circuits, including most of the British tracks. Here is how Sheene tackled Ricard's challenges on a six speed Fabergé Racing 500 cc factory Suzuki, on which at times he reached 180 mph.

Let us start from the straight in front of the big pit's complex. Imagine I am doing a flying lap, so at this point I am in fifth gear – but I then drop it back into third for the left- and right-hand 'S' bend, which is very difficult. For this one, I drift out wide onto the left, and then have to get it back for the right again. Assuming I negotiate that one without any problem, I then shift back into fourth before braking very hard for the chicane, which happens to be slightly downhill! I need first gear for this – with a hard right and hard left. And on the exit I will be right over on the right-hand side of the road. However it is necessary to get over to the left as soon as I can to get round another tight right-hander, the Virage de l'Ecole. This is also a first gear point.

Then I nip into second for the long right-hander called Virage de la Sainte-Baume, which is swiftly followed by a very fast left-hander. This is a very important corner, because it leads onto the main straight, and unless I can get the left-hander absolutely right – and fast – I will not achieve a fast lap time.

The main straight seems to go on for years . . . and it can also be very windy too. In fact, it is named the Mistral Straight after the wind. Accelerating up through the gears, I will take sixth before very long. In fact, by the end of the straight, the leading bikes will be reaching speeds in the region of 180 mph – just about as fast as anywhere in Europe!

Naturally I brake very hard for the Courbe de Signes, dropping down to third gear for what is a difficult corner – because you cannot see the outside of the turn as you enter it. You need to trust your memory for this one.

Exiting from the corner, I will go up one gear, and go over the brow of the hill without lifting, changing down again for a double right-hand bend, probably the most difficult on the whole circuit. It is off camber, downhill, and I need second gear – but have to come down to first for the left and right chicane.

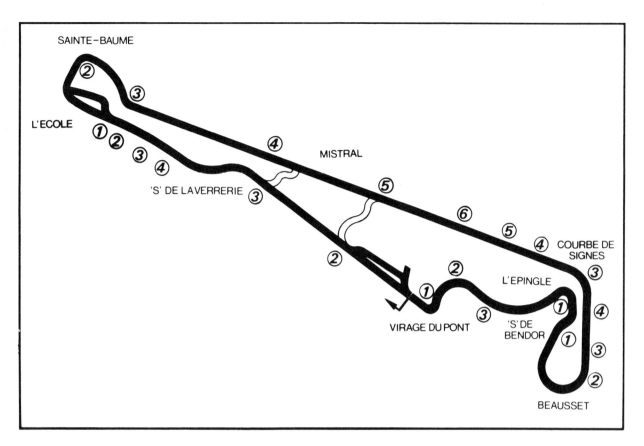

SAINTE-BAUME

L'ECOLE

'S' DE LAVERRERIE

MISTRAL

COURBE DE SIGNES

L'EPINGLE

VIRAGE DU PONT

'S' DE BENDOR

BEAUSSET

Barry Sheene's gearchange guide to Circuit Paul Ricard, France

The next little section, back to the start, is a useful place to make up time, particularly if you become involved in a final sprint to the finishing line.

First, there is a sharp left-hander called L'Epingle, which is immediately followed by a long right-hander, through which I will accelerate and take third gear. But while I am still cranked over to the right, I will have to brake and then change direction to lay it over for the next left-hander, the Virage de la Tour, which requires second gear.

Next, I will dive back across the road to clear the very tight right-hander before the pits. This calls for first gear and a tight line so that I can be in as straight a line as possible for maximum acceleration – and a wheelie or two while accelerating away. It keeps the pits entertained at least!

Circuit Van Drenthe, Assen

From the custom-made, specially constructed racing circuit, we move to a more traditional track, Assen in Holland, the home of the Dutch Grand Prix and other TT motorcycle races – 4.796 miles of closed roads that are normally in everyday use by the public. Here is the champion's guide to lapping the Circuit Van Drenthe, which annually attracts a crowd of around 150,000 motorcycle racing enthusiasts.

Assen is hard work all the time; there is just no time to relax at all. Zooming past the pits on a flying lap, I will be changing up the box – and will take fifth gear on my 500 cc Suzuki before the foot-bridge. The first challenge is the left-hand kink and, after several rides at this track, I finally managed to screw myself up to go through this one flat out – absolutely flat on the tank. This takes some doing on a quick bike, but it is one spot where you can really make up time, although it is obviously very important to be fully aware of your bike's handling so that you can do this in safety.

I take sixth gear after the kink – and then come all the way down the box again for the

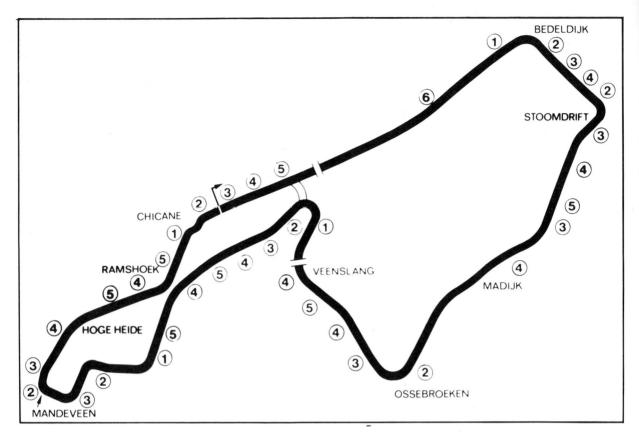

BEDELDIJK

STOOMDRIFT

MADIJK

OSSEBROEKEN

VEENSLANG

HOGE HEIDE

RAMSHOEK

CHICANE

MANDEVEEN

*Barry Sheene's
gearchange guide to
Circuit Van Drenthe,
Assen*

very tight right-hander at the end of the straight called Bedeldijk. Because the straight is so fast, you are pulling a very high gear, therefore first is only just low enough to get round it. It is difficult to get a quick bike's engine turning over fast enough for the power to be available coming out of this one and, early in the race, with a full load of fuel on board, the quicker riders need to slip their clutches during this corner.

There is a left-hand kink on the straight to Stoomdrift – but I accelerate up the box to fourth gear before coming down again to second for the corner itself. Accelerating out of this corner, I take third gear, then fourth, round a left-hand kink and into a difficult left- and right-hand corner.

After that, it is up to fifth, but only briefly, before going down the box again to third for Madijk – the most difficult corner on the circuit.

Immediately after it, I take fourth and negotiate a left-hand kink, then a right-hand kink, and then another left-hand one. I drift out of this last kink on the far right-hand side of the road, but need to get back over to the left again to tackle the slow right-hander called Ossebroeken, a second gear corner.

Along the next section, the front wheel is

only just on the deck . . . and the bike is really twitching. It can be quite a fight to keep it on the road. For you are pulling the bike one way, and accelerating up through third, fourth and fifth – it is hard work.

Then it is down to fourth gear again for the fast right-hander, where a lot of ground can be made up. Immediately after that, there is a slow first-gear corner. Accelerating away from this one, you weave past the back of the pits, the bike often becoming quite a handful at this point. Very soon you are back up into fourth gear for the right, left, another double right and another left – where the circuit meets up with itself.

It is then up to fifth again, before coming all the way down the box to first gear for the hairpin. This one is not so tight and a quick bike can exit cleanly under power. However, you do need to straighten it up as quickly as you can, keeping the front wheel from flapping in the air too much – as you need to point it in the right direction to make a right, left and then a right kink, which all happen in very quick succession. In fact, if you align the bike correctly, you can almost treat them as a straight line before you need to cope with a tight left-hander called Stekkenwal.

I accelerate out of this one, momentarily

up into third, and then down into second for a double right-hander. If you judge this one correctly, you keep the same line without making two corners of it.

Then, it is up into third, and then into fourth for a very fast right-hander, Hoge Heide. Back up to fifth, one more right-hand kink, then there is a left-hand kink before the left-hander where the circuit almost meets itself again. And here you have to brake, change gear and lay the bike over — all at the same time! This is another very important corner at Assen.

Putting on the power again, it is up to fifth gear before going down again to first for the new chicane, which is about the last thing you can do with at this point. For after working pretty hard all the way round the track, you need a rest. Instead, it is hard left, hard right and hard left again.

And that is just one exhausting lap of it.

Superbike trilogy — Sheene, Suzuki, sheer style

A champion's machine

Barry Sheene's Japanese factory-built but British prepared Suzuki 500 cc racing bike produces a giant-sized 120 bhp at 11,000 rpm. On hectic and necessary occasions, such as when Stevie Baker's Yamaha has been in front, 11,500 rpm on the rev counter is not uncommon.

The four-cylinder engine has a square configuration, in that the 50 mm bore and stroke for each cylinder is identical. The engine is a water-cooled two-stroke, a 20:1 petrol to oil mixture of up to 31.5 litres capacity being consumed via a quartet of 34 mm Mikuni variable choke carburettors. The radiator is fitted at the front of the engine, the crankcase of which is made out of magnesium, the bolts from titanium – for low weight and high strength.

The Suzuki factory rider has six constant-mesh gears to change, the air-cooled clutch being made of sintered-bronze, the drive to the rear wheel being by a chain.

Suspension at the front is by air forks with hydraulic dampers; the diameter of the forks have had to be increased to withstand the collossal strains of braking hard from speeds as high as 170 mph or more. At the back, Suzuki's 'golden shot' system is employed with Kayaba shock absorbers, which are damped by gas, air and oil. Race development has again necessitated modifications at the back too, in that the rear arms have had to be braced to prevent their twisting under the sort of acceleration stresses that such an engine is capable of producing.

The brakes are hydraulically actuated front and back – and are both of the disc brake type. At the front, there are twin stainless steel and self-aligning 290 mm diameter discs, and at the back, a single cast-iron ventilated 230 mm diameter disc brake. The wheels are alloy; the tyres are racing ones, either slick at the back in the dry or treaded for wet conditions.

The team take along no less than three different types of fairing to every meeting; fairings which have been developed in a wind tunnel to achieve the ideal of producing the minimum amount of drag but the worst possible conditions behind the bike – to foil the slip-streaming efforts of rivals!

One of the fairings has a flip-up tail to aid rear wheel adhesion and traction; another has a boat tail for ultra-fast circuits where sheer straight line speed is going to count. The rider has the final say which fairing he wants to use for the race, after he has had a chance in practice to try out all the alternatives.

Poetry in motion

There is probably nothing quite so ballet-like as the road racer in action, deftly snicking up and down the gearbox, squeezing the last bhp out of his engine, cranking his steed hard over, this way and that, flowing from bend to bend.

It is undoubtedly a rare and very special combination of the physical and the mechanical. Maybe this is why racing a motorcycle is the most thrilling and yet possibly the most difficult of all motorized sports. Certainly, once you have seen the Duke, Surtees, Hailwood or Sheene, you will have seen a master in action. It is a high-speed balancing act of supreme precision. If you are an enthusiast, like me, you will always remember it, savouring over many, many seasons its very special charisma. The top racers certainly deserve their legends.

Barry Sheene MBE – *the sport's World Champion ambassador*

Stevie Baker – studious, but ruthless; do not be fooled by the specs

Kenny Roberts – super-cool whatever the pace

Johnny Cecotto – a natural, born on a motorcycle

Sidecar Racing

Sidecar racing has evolved a very long way indeed from the early racing of solos with sidecars attached. These days, the highly specialized 'chairs' are all custom-built outfits, very often along entirely different lines of interpretation. The only common denominator is the regulation that racing chairs should have three wheels and carry two people; it is finding the most efficient way of achieving this that gives the most ample scope to the budding designer. For the crowds at the tracks, the chairs add vital variety to the long list of solo races. The machines are of different classes according to engine capacity, and the sidecar racing circus competes in classes, usually up to 500 cc in the world championship, as well as up to the 1300 cc limit permitted for British events and non-championship internationals.

The overall governing regulations, however, do insist that certain dimensional minimum and maximum measurements are adhered to, such as the centres of the bike's wheels being not less than 4 feet apart, and not more than 5 feet 5 inches. The chair itself may be mounted on either side of the bike. The overall width of the outfit's track must not be less than 2 feet 6 inches nor exceed 4 feet. Even the sidecar bodywork has to conform to minimum dimensions of 20 inches high, 20 inches wide and 60 inches long. The streamlined fairing employed must not over-hang the bike by more than 1 foot 6 inches or the sidecar wheel by more than 6 inches, and must end not more than 1 foot 6 inches in front of, or behind the centres of, the various wheel spindles.

Most newcomers to chair racing start off with somebody else's previously raced and so ready-constructed outfit, sensibly buying second-hand, and only branching out into do-it-yourself construction when the rather strange rudiments of the game have been mastered. A wise plan of action, as sidecar racing is so completely different from any other type of motorcycle sport.

The ACU stipulate that the engine must be positioned in the outfit so that it does not protrude beyond a line drawn longitudinally and midway between the wheel tracks made by the rear wheels of the motorcycle and sidecar. Only rear wheel (motorcycle rear wheel, that is) drive is permitted. Sensibly, the ACU have some-thing to say on ground clearance also: it cannot go below 3 inches nor above 12 inches when the outfit is both fuelled and peopled by rider and passenger. As for the brave passenger's accommodation, the rules state that 'he must always be protected from the road wheels and both primary and final drives'. This is only common sense, after all!

There is certainly ample scope for the aerodynamicist to fabricate the most wind-cheating shape of fairing possible. In recent years, the rounded 'dustbin' type of fairing that superseded the 'naked' bike and chair days has been increasingly challenged – and beaten – by the 'wedge-shape' look, which is theoretically more penetrating.

However, whatever style of fairing is adopted, it must not project forward by more than 12 inches beyond the most forward part of the front tyre, while the rearward section must not project rearwards of the rearmost part of the rear tyre by more than 12 inches. The maximum height of the bodywork behind the outfit's rider cannot rise above 35 inches from the ground. The three competition numbers required have to be dimensionally similar to those needed for racing solos – but

What happened to sidecars? They race. Hold tight!

with white figures on black backgrounds.

Perhaps the best thing about sidecar racing is that there is always an extra pair of hands to share the burning of the midnight oil, helping to prepare the mighty machine for race day, and being potentially invaluable at the meeting in the paddock too. On and off the track, sidecar racing calls for a team effort, both competitors having to be thoroughly involved – and also totally dependent on each other's actions. However, the costs are higher than those for racing solos, and the prize money, to offset the costs, very much less – even for the most important events.

Anachronistic? Perhaps. But it is, nonetheless, a very important side to the sport for spectators and competitors alike. Even though the sidecar has all but disappeared from the public roads (apart from the few 'revivalists' who have taken to the roads, one suspects, more for nostalgic reasons than for any practical consideration), racing sidecars have survived – and will carry on surviving because they are, without a doubt 'the fastest chairs in the world'.

The main objectives for the charioteers, apart from being as efficient as possible in accelerating, gearchanging, braking and using the optimum racing line round the track, are to aid traction and streamlining as much as possible. Obviously both are influenced by the occasional transference of rider and passenger weights over the rear tyre, and by both heads keeping well down whenever possible behind the fairing's screens on both bike and chair. In addition, the outfit rider will need to be adept at correcting slides by steering into them, very much as he might if he were driving a four-wheel racing car. The passenger also needs to be blessed with exceptional balance as he quickly moves his weight to keep the sidecar wheel on the deck one minute and aid the rear wheel's traction the next. He must remember to hang on, too.

Jeff Gawley on Sidecar Racing

Jeff Gawley has been an award-winning star of the highly specialized sidecar racing circus for about 15 years. Although his pipework welding business in Scunthorpe demands that he spends more and more time at home, he certainly served his time of the European Grand Prix trail for several seasons and, through continuing with weekend racing forays in Britain, has his name firmly in the sport's record book as a national champion.

The Gawley success story is typical, for it illustrates the amount of dedication that is required to go racing at all, let alone reaching the top. How did this South Humberside engineer become interested in what is the most unusual of all the various branches of motorcycle sport?

I have been interested in bikes for as long as I can remember; I suppose it is the same with most competitors. For I first became involved with a love for bikes as a lad. I used to cycle to Cadwell Park, some 40 miles away, but I always considered it was well worth it. Even then, it was the sidecars which interested me the most. I thought I would like to have a go at sidecar racing one day, and, before very long, I did.

Having left school, I became an apprentice welder with British Steel and, by the time I was 20, I felt I could afford to have a go at racing rather than spectating. It was quite a struggle. But then, in racing, whatever type of machine or class of racing you enter, it usually is.

I started off with a second-hand Vincent racing sidecar chassis from Peter Russell, a regular competitor in those days, using a Vincent Black Shadow motor from my road bike. The intention was that my brother was to join me as passenger. However, it did not work at all well, for he fell out of the chair in practice at the very first meeting, and said 'Never again!' Fortunately, a welding colleague, David Parkinson, took his place, and

we formed a successful team from then on.

One big problem with sidecar racing is that the only way to practise is to actually race. It is not really like any other type of motorcycling, for a roadgoing sidecar is not the same thing as a racer at all. So to learn how to ride and to passenger an outfit, you need to go racing. It is possible to take part in a weekday practice session at several of the circuits, and this is obviously the thing to do if you are a complete newcomer. But there is certainly no substitute for plenty of race laps to find out exactly how to control an outfit and develop the sort of confidence you need to work as a team at speed.

I next replaced the faithful old Vincent with a BSA, and tried to enter as many national and international meetings as my limited funds would allow. However, I always wanted to race abroad, and in 1971, equipped with a BMW, I finally did, even though I did have to give up my job to do it. It is a very strange, nomadic life, travelling from track to track. I had a van and a caravan in tow for the first season on the road, but halfway through the following year, although I could afford to return to Britain to race in the TT, I did not have enough money to get back to the Continent again for the Dutch TT at Assen immediately afterwards. In fact I had to sell the caravan to keep going that year, and lived in a tent for the rest of the season!

However, as a result of making such sacrifices, I was placed fifth in the 1973 World Championships. It was a very good year, with seconds in the French, Austrian, Belgian and Swedish Grand Prix. I would have finished even higher up the championship table if I had not lost second place in the German Grand Prix due to the battery going flat just two laps from the end, and if I had not been forced to drop out at Brno, in Czechoslovakia, with a broken shock absorber — when leading!

The following year was not so successful, even though I switched to a German Konig motor in place of the BMW unit. For apart from a fourth place in Austria, I never really hit the form of the previous season. At the end of the year I decided to stop racing. I did not race at all the next season, and concentrated on my welding partnership in Scunthorpe instead. Yet after a year away from the track, I found I missed racing very

much; it had become such a part of my life. So I put a Yamaha-powered outfit together in 1976, and, despite not racing in every round, I still managed to win second place in the British championship. I was back into racing again, albeit at weekends and only in Britain. Having enjoyed racing for so long, it was too difficult to stop altogether.

However, sidecar racing has become staggeringly expensive these days. My current Castrol-backed outfit has cost about £5,500, and my 750 racing Yamaha motor is itself worth over £3,000. The running spares are also quite costly, and if I wanted to tackle the world championship, I would need a 500 cc motor as well. The sidecar racer needs sufficient capital, plenty of enthusiasm, and a good team around him. I have been very lucky with my passenger, Ken Birch, and my mechanic, Norman Bontoft. The sidecar game is very much a team one. The driver needs the usual skills: judgment, quick reactions, mechanical sympathy, and great attention to detail in the outfit's preparation. He must also have trust in his passenger. The passenger in turn needs to trust his driver, be physically fit, very nimble on his feet, and have faultless balance.

Production Bike Racing

British classic: Norton Commando

From showroom to starting grid

If you want to enter a bike in a production machine race, then for all meetings held under an ACU national permit, the official line is that only motorcycles manufactured during the five-year period prior to 1 January each year – and complying with their definition of a sports motorcycle for 'production machine' races – are eligible. The rules state that the bike must be fully equipped, and must have been built from new components by a motorcycle manufacturer who is recognized as such by the ACU, in the case of the few British firms still existing, or by the equivalent national body in the case of a foreign country of manufacture.

Then the manufacturer, or his concessionaire, must homologate with the ACU, before 1 March each year, the full price and specification of the motorcycle, together with details of all optional extras which could be fitted to the machine before it leaves the factory in the first instance. Such a separate specification is needed for each year's model too. This has to be done by the manufacturer or concessionaire – not the retail dealer. No part of the machine's specification, or indeed any part of its optional extras, are allowed if the bike has been modified in such a way as to have become technically illegal for public road use.

To prevent manufacturers contravening the spirit of these rules and introducing specially-built one-offs masquerading as 'production' sports machines, the regulations insist on there being no less than 200 machines manufactured of all particular models equipped with the listed optional components, and on the bikes being offered for sale to the public through the normal trade channels.

The original specification can be altered, but only when the modifications that are used are employed on the manufacturer's home market, either for earlier or later models. However, the machine from which the modification has come must be listed as being the same type or model, and the modified parts can only be incorporated if it is possible to simply exchange one part for another. Certainly brazing, welding or machining to facilitate the incorporation of home-brewed modifications are not permitted.

The lighter equipment cannot be discarded, nor can the speedometer or the electric starter, if fitted. Even the standard silencing equipment must be retained. Indeed, the bike must not vary from the manufacturer's specification, as homologated with the ACU, in respect of: frame (which must remain completely standard); the rear suspension system (other than the damper units themselves, which can be exchanged for competition specification units); the front forks and suspension; the wheels hubs and brakes (although competition lining material is permitted here); the diameter of the exhaust pipe and the silencing equipment; the primary chain case; the electrical equipment (all of which must be in working order at the start of the race); the carburettors (whose quantity, make, type, model, choke size and fitting, as listed for the motor's original specification, only can be used – a carburettor listed as an optional extra cannot); the oil tank capacity (and its material and method of attachment to the machine); the type of engine, number of cylinders and stroke (although the bore may be increased – provided the increase does not result in exceeding the limits of the original capacity class as registered with the ACU); the crankcase; the cylinder head casting (and the material used); the operating system of the induction and the exhaust; the type of gearbox (including the number of speeds); the clutch (again, apart from the lining material used as well as the springs); and the type of primary and secondary transmission. Only the air filter elements can be removed.

However, in the interests of safety, or to suit the preference of the rider, some equipment may be varied, mainly the exhaust pipes, as long as the diameter remains as originally supplied with the machine, and the line of pipe is not varied to increase ground clearance. The original pattern of silencer must be retained, and the shape must not be altered at all. You are not even allowed to make 'flats' on the silencers to increase the ground clearance when the machine is leaned over for cornering. However, any shape of handlebars is permitted, provided the original method of attachment is retained. All wheel rims can be changed, and the petrol tank can be substituted for another one, as long as its capacity is no smaller than 6 litres and no larger than 24.

Certain changes to the original specification are mandatory, being quite obviously in the interests of the rider's safety. Bolt-on rear number plates and tail lamp assemblies (where they are part of the number plate assembly), the licence holder, centre and prop stands as well as luggage carriers and trafficators, can all be discarded.

The stop lamps can either be disconnected or removed altogether. However, the headlamp glass and rear lamp cover, if fitted, must be protected by tape or similar material – to avoid splintering glass getting onto the track and possibly cutting somebody's tyres. Racing tyres are encouraged. If road tyres are used, they must be at least 'H and V' rated. 'Production machine' rules also allow the addition of security bolts to prevent the tyre covers moving round on the rims.

Full or nosecone fairings are allowed, as are steering dampers. As for any other part not specifically mentioned in the 'thou shalt not modify' category above, these can be modified to suit the individual preference of the rider, but only if the part concerned was supplied as part of the original manufacturer's specification.

Formula TT

The ultimate form of production bike racing, in ACU parlance, is 'Formula TT', where the rules state that the motorcycle has to be in current production, and also be on sale through normal commercial channels. Once again the ACU demand that, before 1 March each year, proof is furnished to them that at least 200 machines of a certified model have actually been sold to the public.

The bikes have to be presented for racing with all their electrical equipment as originally supplied and in working order. No changes are permitted to the type of engine, the number of cylinders or the stroke. The materials and castings (of which the cylinder, cylinder head, crankcase and gearbox are made) must be original. You cannot change the number, type and size of carburettor. However, the number of gears can be altered, provided that no changes are made to the actual gearbox casing itself.

Petrol tank capacity limits vary according to the four main cubic capacity classes for a permitted tank change of up to 15 litres capacity for TT Formula IV, 18 litres for TT Formula III, 20 litres for TT Formula II and 24 litres for TT Formula I. A change of tank from the standard unit is therefore permitted as long as the new one conforms to these maximum capacities.

The cubic capacity divisions for two-strokes are as follows: over 50 cc, up to

125 cc, TT Formula IV; over 125 cc, up to 250 cc, TT Formula III; over 250 cc, up to 350 cc, TT Formula II; over 350 cc, up to 500 cc, TT Formula I. For four-strokes the divisions are: over 50 cc, up to 200 cc, TT Formula IV; over 200 cc, up to 400 cc, TT Formula III; over 400 cc, up to 600 cc, TT Formula II; over 600 cc, up to 1000 cc, TT Formula I. Formula TT competitors can increase the bore of their engines as long as the pattern of the cylinder is not changed, and provided that this increase in capacity does not result in the limits being exceeded for the class for which the machine has originally been registered.

Modification to the exhaust system (as well as the silencers) is permitted in order to satisfy safety measures, but the maximum noise level is fixed at 115 decibels, which is measured at an average piston speed of 13 metres/seconds for two-strokes and 11 metres/seconds for four-strokes. On multi-cylinder machines, the noise levels are measured on each cylinder's exhaust outlet or pair of cylinder's exhaust outlets.

Once again, in the interest of safety, the Formula TT rules allow riders to remove their bike's electrical equipment – the lights, indicators, horn and so forth, as well as the numberplates, speedometer, and indeed any other items that may be listed in an event's 'supplementary regulations'.

A relative amount of freedom is permitted when it comes to boring the machine out (within the maximum cubic capacity of the class, of course), increasing the valve sizes and the camshaft lift as well as changing the shape of the combustion chambers and opening out the ports. And as long as the 'type of engine' is the same, you are even allowed to fit a stronger crankshaft.

The Isle of Man TT course – the home of purist road racing; sadly, some say, just about its last remaining bastion, too

The national governing body for motorcycle sport (in Britain the ACU) has to produce 'Certificates of Homologation' for Formula TT models, indicating that they comply with the various requirements. It is these 'certificates' which represent the authority for the motorcycle to take part in Formula TT racing.

6 Sprinting and Drag Racing

The essential difference between a sprint and a drag race meeting is between time and elimination. At a sprint, a rider puts himself against the clock, whereas a drag competitor is really only concerned with beating any other rider who is paired to run with him.

In sprints, the awards go to whoever the electronic timing device determines has been the fastest over the course – in various maximum cubic capacity engine classes, in the usual way.

In drag racing, the winner is the rider who has beaten each of the rivals who have been drawn to race against him from the start line to the other end of the 'drag strip' in a series of 'eliminators', actually not necessarily putting the fastest time up in the class by doing so.

In both forms of the sport, competitors set off from a standing start, the sprinter starting in his own turn, the drag racer being started by a complicated 'Christmas tree' set of special starting lights. Sprinters invariably ride down the course alone, drag racers two at a time. As a result, traditional sprints are essentially of more interest to participants, while the newer and American-inspired drag racing events are quite naturally more likely to appeal to spectators. However, both types of competition involve a straight-line course on tarmac, usually being of a measured quarter of a mile, although sprint rules permit a maximum of one mile.

The ACU insist that competitors have competition licences of the correct grade – and present both their machines and the usual mandatory protective clothing to a scrutineer before being allowed to practise.

In sprints, the various class divisions range from a class of up to 125 cc to classes of over 1300 cc, and over 2000 cc. In drag racing, only bikes of over 240 cc are catered for. In the bigger classes, there is the most scope for 'creativity', for unsupercharged two-wheel monsters are welcome in the 2001 to 3500 cc class!

Sprint bikes
The modifications can be fairly extensive; most bikes tend to be either cast-off circuit racing machines, or motorcycles specifically constructed for efficient standing starts, acceleration and straight-line speed. However, the rules still insist that both solos and outfits must not take lightening to the extreme – sprint bikes must still be equipped with at least two brakes. The type of tyre that can be used is relatively free of restriction, apart from the sensible stipulation that the front tyre's cross-section must not be too skinny, and must be no less than 2 inches.

Clutch and brake levers, once again, have to be ball-ended, even if the machine is genuinely old. The drive and primary chains have to be adequately guarded to prevent accidental contact on any part of their runs between sprockets. Mudguards can be discarded. Unlike circuit racing, streamlining is not only permitted but the shape that can be used is also free of restriction, and even solos are able to use full 'dustbin' fairings. The only rule is that there has to be 2 inches of clearance between the fairing and the ends of the bars.

Supercharging of the engine is permitted, and it does not affect the engine class for which the bike's cubic capacity qualifies. Also, unless specifically stated in the event's supplementary regulations, there is no restriction as to the type of fuel that may be used.

In the largest solo engine class, namely 1300 to 2000 cc, an on–off ignition cut-out switch, very much like that accepted in car racing, has to be fitted in an accessible position on the handlebars, so that it can be operated in an emergency by the rider, or even by a marshal.

The regulations also demand that a final drive steel guard, with a minimum thickness of $\frac{1}{16}$ inch steel or $\frac{1}{8}$ inch alloy gauge, must be fitted to enclose the top run if a chain is used, or restraining steel rings fitted, one at each end, if shaft-drive is employed. A clutch guard must also be fitted, and must be of sufficient strength to protect the rider if the clutch should disintegrate.

Bearing in mind the fact that this is the class in which competitors will be running elongated frames to accommodate more than one engine, the front steering assembly must have a minimum trail of 4 inches and, in the scrutineer's opinion, it must be of sufficient strength to obviate any likelihood of collapse, either during acceleration or under braking conditions. Flimsy forks or excessively light-weight frames are unlikely to be permitted by the scrutineer.

For sprint events, a colour system for the competition number plates of the various classes applies: up to 125 cc – white numbers on red background; over 125 to 250 cc – white numbers on green background; over 250 to 350 cc – white numbers on blue background; over 350 to 500 cc – black numbers on yellow background; over 500 to 750 cc – black numbers on red background; over 750 to 1000 cc – black numbers on white background; over 1000 to 1300 cc – black numbers on white background; and over 1300 to 2000 cc – black numbers on white background.

Unlike circuit racing, a passenger need not be carried in the sidecar category, ballast being permitted instead – to a weight of not less than 132 pounds. The main three-wheeler sprint classes are up to 500 cc, and over 500 up to 1300 cc, and white competition numbers on black backgrounds are required.

Drag bikes

There is no provision for sidecars in drag events. Solos are catered for in three basic divisions, according to their state of modification, and are further sub-divided into seven classes, according to the cubic capacity of their engines. The three divisions are: 'S' for Street, open to all motorcycles which are taxed, insured and legally allowed to drive the streets (proof being required); 'PS' for Pro Street, open to all road-based but highly modified solo motorcycles; and 'C' for Competition, open to all motorcycles designed and constructed for out-and-out racing.

The capacity classes in drag events are: 'F', 240 to 350 cc; 'E', 351 to 500 cc; 'D', 501 to 750 cc; 'C', 751 to 1000 cc; 'B', 1001 to 1200 cc; 'A', 1301 to 2000 cc; and 'AA', 2001 to 3500 cc, but unsupercharged. At a meeting, a competitor will be identified not only by his competition number but by both the capacity classification and division letters; for example 'ES 99' indicates a 500 cc Street solo number 99.

The things people will dream up to get a quick time, a Triple Triumph 650 – blown!

Street solos can only use a commercial grade of fuel that is supplied to the public from any forecourt. The normal and road-going lighting equipment must be retained, although the lens/light unit may be removed for safety – if it is not, then it should be protected by tape or a plastic cover. Mudguards must be fitted too, to comply with the Road Traffic Act. The stand must be wired up or removed

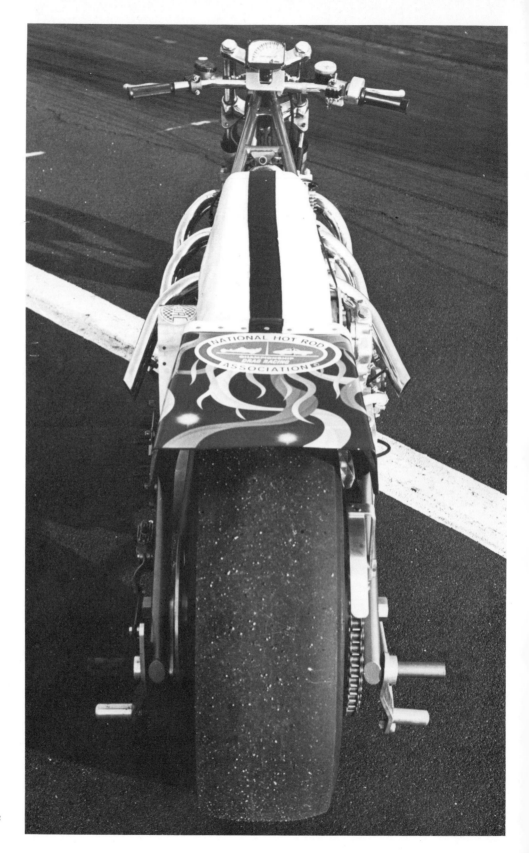

*Built strictly for
straight lines – with
lots of rubber to burn
and no tread*

The shortest and fastest two wheel kick going – with the most G too

altogether, so that it cannot fall down during a run. However, a supercharger cannot be fitted. Although any type of motorcycle wheel is allowed, the tyres must be ordinary road-going ones of reputable manufacture, and with a minimum tread depth of 2 mm. In other words, bikes in this division must be genuine road-going machines.

Pro Street competitors can modify their mounts much more extensively. The rules for this division allow any make or type of camshaft to be fitted. Any make or type – and in any combination – of carburation or fuel injection may be installed too. The ignition, clutch and gearbox can be subjected to unlimited modification. A supercharger is allowed. However, once again a normal commercial brand of fuel that is available from any forecourt is the only type of fuel permissible. The engine, although extensive modifications are permitted, must be based upon a road-going motorcycle engine that is generally available.

A different frame can be used, as long as it is based upon one that is generally available from a reputable frame manufacturer. Any alterations or modifications can be made to any of the mountings or brackets attached to the frame in order to accommodate the engine and ancillary equipment installation. However the steering head angle must be 65°, plus or minus 10 per cent.

Open exhaust systems are permitted for Pro Street bikes, but square profile 'slick' tyres are not. Patterned racing tyres can be used, as long as they comply with the minimum tread rule of 2 mm and the minimum front tyre width of 2.75 inches. The other crucial dimension is the wheelbase, which should not exceed the 65 inches maximum rule.

The Competition Solo division allows for machines to be specially constructed for drag racing. Virtually anything goes too. There is no limit, even on the number of engines that can be used, although, quite obviously, transmission chains and supercharger drive belts have to be very adequately guarded with shields.

Any suitable road or racing type or size of tyre can be employed, a 'slick' being the usual equipment for the back wheel – if dry. Even the fuel can be different in this class, since there is no limitation on the type of fuel, apart from hydrazine not being permitted.

The start line

Whether sprint or drag race riding, the three main essentials are obvious enough: to leave the line as quickly as the equipment will permit you to do; to fully utilize the engine's power characteristics, but to change gear super-efficiently; and to

John Hobbs, Drag Superstar, blasts off to achieve space-age acceleration times

try to make the profile of the machine as aerodynamically clean as possible by keeping right down behind the fairing's screen, as far as is humanly practical. This may sound easy enough, just like roaring away from another set of lights. However, the slightest fumble and, in a competitive class, your time will be unplaced; while in a drag event, a poor time might mean your 'elimination', and therefore no chance to make a second, mistake-free run.

At least with a sprint you can start when you are absolutely ready – once you have been given the starter's signal, of course. Even so, you must ensure that you start cleanly and purposefully, because, just as soon as you break the timing beam, your time will have started. However for a drag race start you have to be poised to go just as soon as the column of lights hits the bottom of the 'Christmas tree'. Although you do not want to become preoccupied with whatever your rival competitor is – or is not – doing alongside you, you still need to be steering a straight course and staying in your own lane. Obviously, you will need to make allowances for crosswinds. If you are eventually going to graduate to a really wild machine, you will need to indulge in such specialities as warming up the rear tyre's rubber to make it more 'grippy'.

Finally, whatever the bike, ideally both the engine and gearbox oil should be warmed up. Whatever the engine's size or state of tune, you will need to drive the strip with the rev counter very much in sight, as some of the faster quarter-milers are crossing the finishing line in well under ten seconds, by which time they could be doing over 90 miles an hour!

7 Grass Track

Dicing on the Turf

Grass track racing is quite simply what it implies – motorcycle racing but on a grass circuit. The difference between it and motocross is that the grass track racer's field of battle is supposed to be relatively flat and much smoother. However, in practice, riding quickly on grass can be extremely hard work for a rider, and can call for a considerable amount of physical fitness to set up and hold the bike in a speedway-style drift through the corners. For once the top grass has been worn off, even though the dirt beneath could be described as loose surface, trying to make the bike slide is, surprisingly, very much harder work than broadsiding round the artificial shale of a stadium.

As with nearly all the other branches of two-wheeled sport, the competitive grass track bike has also evolved into rather a special animal. Any motorcycle can be used, subject to compliance with the special regulations governing the sport. But in order to win, you need a proper grass track bike, or a slightly modified speedway machine. For national and above status grass track meetings, just as in speedway, brakes can be dispensed with altogether. However, for typical British restricted events, this sport's regulations insist on solo bikes having at least one brake operating on the rear wheel, and sidecar outfits having at least two braked wheels.

Except for the prohibited use of tractor-type tyres and studded or spiked ice racing tyres, which could all too easily destroy the track's surface, there is no restriction as to the type of tyre which may be used. To protect the rider, two mudguards must be fitted, the rear one having to cover at least 45° of the upper rear quadrant of the rear wheel. If a roadgoing 'off-road' bike, or similar, is being used, all the lamps, the number plate and so forth must be removed, again for safety reasons.

Noise is being increasingly policed. The ACU can carry out spot checks at meetings and exclude any rider whose machine exceeds their 110 decibels limit; this is determined by the FIM system of placing a microphone 1.5 m from each exhaust outlet at an angle of 45° from the rear end (or above, on complicated sidecar installations) of the centre line of the motorcycle – and at least 0.2 m above the ground. Meanwhile, the bike's engine mean piston speed for such a test has to be 13 m/sec, which the organizers work out according to the machine's cubic capacity by clocking up the calculated number of rpm on the rev counter.

In fact, organizers of grass track racing in Britain have become so concerned over the noise problem, lest they lose venues as a result of complaints from the local inhabitants, that they even prohibit competitors from running their engines, on penalty of exclusion from the meeting, except during official practice and the actual racing itself, plus a period not exceeding five minutes prior to the start of each race.

The largest capacity class allows machines of over 500 and up to 1300 cc, where the competition numbers have to be in black on white backgrounds, one at the front and one on each side. The other classes are: over 350 up to 500 cc, black numbers on yellow backgrounds; over 250 up to 350 cc, white numbers on blue backgrounds; over 125 up to 250 cc, white numbers on green backgrounds; over 100 but under 125 cc, white numbers on black backgrounds; and the smallest

A grass track duel of 'the Titans': Peter Collins rides round the outside of Ivan Mauger (it worked, Collins won)

solo class of all, 50 cc, where competitors must use black numbers on white competition plates. The maximum engine capacity permitted in sidecar races is 1000 cc, supercharging being permitted up to 650 cc, and three-wheelers having to carry white competition numbers on black background plates.

The layout of the normally oval track is often varied for sidecar competitions; a chicane is usually inserted halfway down one of the straights. The lap distance at British venues varies from 400 metres (a pair of straights connecting two equally radiused corners) to 800 metres round the longest tracks. In the more popular classes, competitors qualify by putting up successful performances in a series of heats before entering the class final.

Grass track racing and sand racing have the same set of rules, as the machines required and the riding techniques involved are very similar. The flag signals are much the same as in circuit racing.

Apart from being an excellent training ground for speedway riders, grass track racing has become very big in recent years in its own right, attracting big-name sponsors like Bulmers. For the spectators, spectacular riding is virtually guaranteed. For those taking part, the speeds are extremely high, and there are, fortunately, few solid objects to hit in the event of a tumble.

Dust gets in your eye – unless you can lead

Guidelines By Tom Leadbitter

Tom Leadbitter, a bricklayer, was, in common with the vast majority of the male population, soccer mad. His life revolved around football . . . until the early 'sixties, when he stumbled across a motorcycle scramble one Saturday afternoon on TV. He was an instant convert, and before very long became a competitor himself, starting off what has been a long and successful riding career with a 250 cc Villiers-engined DOT.

And yet it has not been in motocross that Leadbitter has really made his mark, nor in speedway either, which he increasingly entered from the end of the sixties – but in grass track racing. For Leadbitter, broadsiding round the field, once seen, is unlikely to be forgotten. Therefore any advice from this grass track professional, who today combines his love of dicing on the turf with professional speedway riding, is certainly worthy of the aspiring participant's attention.

Although there are 250 cc and 350 cc classes in grass track racing, and one would think it better to advise a novice to start off with a smaller bike, in actual fact I would recommend any newcomer to go straight into the bigger 500 cc class. For with the smaller bikes you do not have enough power on tap, certainly not the sort of power you need to ride the grass really quickly.

The basic essential in this branch of the sport is to enter the corners as quickly as you can, so that you can achieve the necessary momentum to come out of them as fast as possible. To be able to extract the most out of your bike, you will need to alter the gearing according to the length of the track's straights – either by altering the rear sprockets, the engine sprocket, or both, so that the engine can pull its maximum rpm for as much of each lap as possible. Although bikes have two-speed gear boxes, the lower ratio is only used to get away from the start – and from then on it is top all the way. However, it is still necessary to vary the main rear wheel sprocket. I use between a 54 and a 56 tooth sprocket as well as a smaller engine one; again mine can vary between a 15 tooth and a 22 tooth version.

A typical British grass track circuit length will be about half a mile round, consisting of two big radius turns connected by a couple of straights of about 200 yards in length, on which the faster bikes will be reaching 75 mph or so. On some of the European tracks, where the lap distances and therefore the straights are very much longer, speeds in the region of 95 mph are possible. What you need to achieve is gearing which will allow you to keep the throttle fully open – without the engine over-revving and blowing up – all the way round the track.

All the corners are left-handers, so the technique is to lean the bike over to the left in the turns, your right foot firmly on the right-hand footrest and the left foot only being used to steady yourself – rather than putting any real weight on it.

You should try to ride round the corners without any wheel spin, with maximum traction – and, as far as the top riders are concerned, with both feet up out of the way. However, in actual fact, when a grass track bike is leaned well over, the machine will tend to break away. So, to go quickly, you should neither lift off the throttle nor dig your left foot in too much. You must equip your left boot with a proper 'slipper' sole made out of steel, and should never run with a conventional heel, which could all too easily catch on the ground and do your leg a great deal of harm.

For international events, the regulations do not permit bikes to have any brakes at all; on British nationals, rear brakes only are mandatory. However, just because they are permitted, it does not mean to say that you should necessarily use them during racing. For if you do – you simply will not win! You should slow down instead by altering the degree of lean or the angle of broadside.

For grass track riding, you need to be fit – fitter even than for speedway. Forcing a bike through a corner on grass can be very hard work indeed, because even after the grass top surface has been worn away and you are down to the earth, this can be absolutely rock hard and, far from being a loose surface, it actually affords staggeringly high grip. This is fine for cutting out time-wasting wheelspin, but not so good if you need to

*No shortage of style –
Gerald Short turns on
all 500 cc, on grass at
Long Marston*

deliberately slide the bike sideways so that you can actually get round another rider or a corner.

You must take what you wear very seriously indeed. Do not make do with just any riding gear. Even though grass tracks are relatively flat, and there are no trees to hit, the ground can still feel as hard as concrete if you come off, and can also do as much damage. Wear a really good one-piece set of leathers, top quality boots and padded leather motocross gloves, as the stones thrown up by other competitors can damage your fingers unless they are protected properly. Full-face or open-face helmets can be worn, but I always favour an open-face one. Inside my leathers I wear a back protector (the sort of thing that National Hunt jockeys wear) and I would not be without it.

The face needs plenty of protection, particularly if you wear an open-faced helmet. I wear a motocross face mask and good goggles. Do not economize with these; after all, you only have one pair of eyes, and you should bear in mind that if a stone is thrown up by another competitor's rear wheel at 60 mph and you are doing another 60 mph on top, the impact speed of the stone into your face could be as much as 120 mph!

I also fit several tear-off lenses over my goggles, so that with one swift hand movement I can very quickly clear muddied-over vision resulting from following another competitor's rear wheel rather closely.

Not long ago, there was very little money to be won on 'the grass'. In recent seasons however the rewards have improved, and £100 for winning the major race at a British national event is common, with additional payments towards travelling expenses and accommodation for the star riders. The big rewards though, certainly in terms of starting money, still lie on the European mainland, where it is possible for a successful rider from British club meetings to race professionally and win. However he would need to combine such outings with speedway, where much more money is paid out.

You can compete quite successfully with only one machine and fairly limited spares, but to be ultra-successful you will need to tie up quite a lot of money in more than one bike and equipment. I have about £8,000 invested in bikes, spare motors and tools, and also need a reliable van to take the equipment to the meetings. So there can be a fairly sizable investment involved.

8 Speedway

Stadium Racing

Of all the different types of motorcycle sport, speedway is the least easy for the participant to break into but, even when compared to circuit racing, it is nonetheless the most popular with spectators. Indeed next to football, speedway racing is the second largest spectator sport in Britain. The reason for its success must be that it is so utterly straightward and uncomplicated. There are no problems of having to work out who has lapped whom, the races being short, sharp and always highly spectacular. Besides, the game involves so little travelling for the fans too, since the tracks are usually close to the population centres. The use of floodlighting enables the racing to be watched in the evening, which is often convenient from the spectator's point of view. Finally, the admission charges are low compared with conventional racing circuit prices.

Apparently, speedway started in the United States in the early 1900s, although Australia often lays claim to being the sport's birthplace. In its early days, particularly in America, it was more of an inter-manufacturer affair, and the individual winner was always much more important than the inter-team competition that has been the sport's backbone in Britain for the last 50 years.

The sport started on tracks that were distinctly improvised, merely being laid out on a stretch of dirt. The surface was fairly rugged, and the lap distance, at a mile round in some cases, was very much longer than we are used to in speedway today. In the early days, although the surface was nearly always 'loose', interestingly riders tended to ride round the track with their feet up on the footrests, the classic foot-steadying broadside not coming in until the early 'twenties.

The first British 'dirt track' event, as opposed to grass track racing where real speedway broadsiding took place, albeit on an experimental demonstration-like basis, was not in fact held until 1927, at Camberley in Surrey. This was followed by the first organized competitions shortly afterwards, both on a cinder track at Droylesden, near Manchester, and on an oval track in Epping Forest a year later. It appears that around this time the sport really took off; regular speedway events roared into life securing mass popularity all over the place, so much so that a 78,000-strong gate was attracted to the June White City meeting in 1928.

From those early days, the number of tracks increased until few cities were without one, the sport owing as much to the gamble of promoters as the pluck of the intrepid competitors. Obviously the sport suffered a decline during the war years, but in the post-war period of the late 'forties speedway enjoyed its all-time height of popularity. At the end of 1949 there were no fewer than 37 tracks open, which logged some 12,500,000 spectator attendances through their turnstiles in the year.

Today, speedway is enjoying an on-going revival from the late 'fifties and early 'sixties, when the crowds and the number of teams declined. However, in more recent seasons, things have been very different and the amount of TV time that the sport has been receiving is surely indicative of the extent of its comeback. At the time of writing, the nation's speedway teams are keenly followed by a very large number of fans indeed. The teams are in two divisions, football-style, making up the British and national leagues, there being the usual sort of soccer system for determining who wins each division, who moves up from 'Division Two' into 'Division One' and who moves down from 'Division One' into 'Division Two', all on the basis of two points for a match win and one for a draw. In each inter-team match, there are likely to be thirteen races of four laps each, with two riders from each team competing for the points, three going for first, two for second and one point for third. The riders are paid according to the points they score, and in addition they also receive starting money. At a typical meeting, the races are run almost continuously, usually at the non-stop rate of one every five minutes or so, the points moving up for each team until a final result is achieved.

A typical team consists of seven riders: the best three are called 'heat leaders', the next two are called 'second strings' and the last two are the 'reserves'. The event's programme is so designed as to give the maximum variation in races, the heat leaders and second strings being programmed for four rides each and the

Speedway: formation dancing – but faster. Only the brave need apply

reserves three. Then if a team falls six points behind, they are allowed to make a 'tactical substitute', which means that they can replace any rider in their team with any other team member. For example, a reserve might be replaced by a heat leader, thus enabling a team to recover – and so stand a chance of regaining some lost points. One of the reserve riders can also be brought into play at any time to replace an off-form heat leader or second string. However, the reserve can only have a total of five rides if he is used in this way.

Four riders, two from each team, race at any one time, starting behind a set of tapes which stretch across the track and rise swiftly upwards when the start referee judges that all the riders are ready and their bikes' engines are running. The tapes are rather similar to the starting gate system used in horse racing. However, if a rider is over-eager and breaks one of the tapes, he is immediately excluded from that particular race and therefore scores no points for his team. The races are always run in an anti-clockwise direction, each race being of four laps' duration. Flags are used to indicate certain essential information to both the riders and the public: yellow with a black cross means one lap to go; chequered means end of race; red means race stopped; black means rider excluded.

Apart from such inter-team matches, there are also individual competition nights, where one rider becomes the outright winner of the event rather than his team. Contests between pairs of riders are organized too.

The speedway bike
In the very early days, roadsters were used for the events, but for as long as the sport has been run along the lines that it is today, a specialist speedway bike has been the competitor's weapon. However, the speedway bike has evolved into an extremely curious machine. The regulations demand that it should have no brakes, the only controls being a clutch and twist-grip throttle. The thinking behind the 'no brakes' rule is that it is safer! It prevents riders who are leading from stopping too quickly and so causing a pile-up with the following riders. Speedway racing tends to be extremely close at times.

In international competitions, the maximum allowed capacity for the engine is 500 cc, although in national events, when all the riders are under agreement to a British promoter, the cubic capacity of the engine must not exceed 510 cc. No supercharging is allowed. The normal specification for the engine used for speedway bikes is single cylinder, four-stroke. In recent years the authorities have become extremely strict about the amount of noise that a bike is allowed to make. A special silencer, one that is stamped as being approved by the British Speedway Promoters Association, has become mandatory. The outlet of the exhaust cannot terminate more than two inches in front or more than two inches to the rear of the rear wheel spindle. Another rule, wisely so, is that there must be adequate primary chain-guarding so that, in the event of an accident, the rider is protected.

The only fuel permitted is pure methanol – and without any demon additives, such as nitro. The use of pure alcohol fuel means that engines will run cooler and so the compression ratio can be raised considerably, many speedway engines running with as much as 15.0:1 compression. This fuel works out at about £1 per gallon, and does not disappear at a faster rate than ordinary pump petrol. However, there is absolutely no opportunity for cheating. For the track's referee can order the inspection of any machine's fuel and can, at random, have samples of the fuel analyzed. Any rider found guilty of using an additive not only has to pay the cost of the analysis but will also be subject to disciplinary proceedings. Speedway riders do not cheat.

Needless to say, the speedway bike is a very functional animal indeed, there being absolutely no surplus weight at all; even the size of the fuel tank is pruned down to the absolute minimum. The left-hand (that is, the inside) footrest is discarded, only one on the right-hand side being necessary. To cope with the shale and crushed granite surfaces that abound on most tracks, speedway bike tyres are controlled too, in that they have to have the ACU approved trials-type tread pattern, and the all-important rear one has to be 19×3.50 inches in size.

Although you do not change gear on a speedway bike, it being permanently fixed according to the size of the track and therefore the length of the straights, the competitor still needs to alter his gearing by changing either or both the engine and rear-wheel sprockets. The stadium track lap distance in Britain can vary between 300 and 450 yards round; quarter-mile circuits are about the longest, and here the speeds at the end of the 100 yard long straights can be over 70 mph.

Since the 'thirties, when the first JA Prestwich engines started to appear, ousting the Douglas Twins from the top placings, the single cylinder engine has been dominant in speedway. Indeed, right up until the early 'sixties when the first ESOs from Czechoslovakia, the forerunners of the current Jawas, started coming onto the scene, the Jap engine was the one to use. Today, even though there are still Jap engines in circulation, Jawas are the most popular choice; the all-British Weslake motor has however been doing much of the winning in recent years, even taking a world championship for Britain.

The original Jawa formula for success was based on straightforward, magneto-sparked, two-valve, single-cylinder motor in light alloy, producing bhp in the low 50s at 7,000 rpm, the usable limit obviously being 1,000 or so revs in excess of this figure. Yet more recently, following on from Weslake's successful revival of using four valves to obtain some 54 bhp, Jawa too have opted for the more complex top end for their latest engines – and as a result the power output of the top bikes for the next few seasons could be some 10 bhp more than this. This figure is quite staggering when you remember that the engines are only half a litre.

And so to race

Speedway racing is very difficult to start. There are no official exploratory schemes available for you to discover whether you are going to like it or not. They do not even have practice sessions at meetings; the vast majority of the riders are already experienced enough to get straight on with the racing. True, the teams do have a few 'practice only' sessions, but these tend to be restricted to their team riders, and are run for the team to try out mechanical adjustments. Fortunately, however, some tracks do run the occasional training session for riders who want to become used to handling speedway bikes for the first time and to break the ice with the necessary riding techniques involved without having to do this actually in a race.

It seems that most of the novices to the sport have come from grass track racing, where they have already mastered the rudiments of power-sliding through corners on loose surfaces to a degree of accuracy. The speedway rider really does need to know exactly what he is doing. He will have to ride in very close proximity to other competitors. It is hardly fair to them if he is still finding out what happens in the corners if he lifts off. So the advice to the aspiring newcomer to this particular branch of the sport must be to go grass track racing first, and then graduate to speedway later on.

In team competitions, there are two riders from each team in each race; the exact starting positions on the grid are determined democratically, so that everybody has the opportunity to enjoy the advantage or otherwise of the inside position. If one teams falls six points behind the other, they are given the sporting chance of being able to choose the starting positions for their pair of riders in each race. However, they cannot select both the inside two lanes: the inside and the third lane, or the second and the outside lane. It also goes without saying that riding round the inside of the track, hugging the inside line through both the corners, although the shortest way round, is not necessarily the fastest. For as the track wears, so too may the fastest line. In other words, the fastest surface can vary and so the traction may be better in the middle of the track or even round the ouside in places. The necessary manoeuvres are, of course, legion – but uncomplicated. Straightforward common sense counts for more than bravado.

A sliding spectacular. No wonder this branch of the sport is 'Top of the Pops' with the crowds

As for the costs involved, these are surprisingly low – as long as you are successful. For there is plenty of prize and starting money as well as sponsorship in speedway these days. Even the most competitive, brand new bike, complete with the latest four-valve engine, is unlikely to cost more than £1,200 (at the time of writing),

while a new two-valve Jawa, all ready to race, could be yours for £750. And as with all other branches of motorcycle sport, the secondhand bargain opportunities are legion, sound buys being obtainable for less than £400. But try grass tracking first – or your money may be wasted.

Advice from Len Silver

Len Silver and speedway have been inseparable for some 30 years. This one-time rider for Ipswich and former captain of Exeter, with whom he enjoyed most of his winning, finally rode for Hackney, where today he is the promoter, after injury stopped his riding career several seasons ago.

Both on and off the track, Silver has seen it all, for speedway has been both his all-consuming hobby and his job too. He has enjoyed a lifetime of speedway racing experience, but nonetheless has always been willing to pass on some of the lessons he has learnt over the years.

Before you contemplate taking up speedway, you must ask yourself whether you really have the necessary attributes to make it. Do you have the necessary motorcycle skills? Are you at home on two wheels, in the same way that some people are instantly happy playing ball games? For being happy on two wheels is one of the basic essentials in successful speedway riding. You also need to be fairly courageous. It can be an extremely dangerous sport at times.

Then, do you have a really good sense of balance? If not, you cannot hope to get anywhere, for, contrary to popular belief, a rider only puts weight on his left leg for less than half a second per corner. All his weight will be on the only footrest – on the right. This is where the balance factor comes into its own.

An analytical brain comes fairly high up on the list of a rider's priorities. There are far more tactics in speedway racing than many people realize. You quite often need to be able to fool another rider into doing things that you want him to do. You will also need to pre-judge what the rest of the riders in your race are likely to do. Very quick reactions are necessary, of course, and so is physical fitness. You do not have to be a giant, nor desperately strong – just fit. In fact, many top speedway riders are quite small, compact chaps.

Good eyesight and hearing are both important too. You do not have any mirrors – and you have to ride very, very close to other riders at times. So you must be able to judge things to the inch sometimes. And if you are in front, you ideally need to be able to hear on which side your rival is trying to pass you.

Finally, self-confidence comes fairly high

on the list, too. All the riders who make it to the top are very, very confident. They totally believe in themselves – arrogant perhaps, but nonetheless it is very necessary to be so.

How do people come into speedway in the first place? Well, these days, there are an increasing number of recruits to the sport who come from junior motorcycling, both from grass track events and schoolboy scrambling. Perhaps surprisingly, few speedway riders seem to come from the ranks of road motorcyclists. In fact, most speedway riders seem to have done most of their motorcycling on speedway bikes, for speedway is so very specialized, that there is absolutely no comparison with road motorcycling.

Most of the larger tracks now hold speedway training days, when it is possible for the novice club member to find out what speedway riding is all about. Some clubs even hire out bikes for this purpose. The local manager will nearly always be in attendance, being on the look-out for potential team rider material.

Even if you have participated in a lot of schoolboy motorcycle sport, you still need to be over 14 to be physically able to handle a speedway bike. It is a very wild and potent machine indeed, with an enormously high power to weight ratio – and no brakes! In fact, a rider has to be over 16 before a promoter can hand out a professional contract.

Once your local club officials consider you are competent, and you have bought your own bike, you will be allowed to take part in a meeting – in the second half of the programme's races to start with. If you show form on such occasions, you might even

Peter Collins, World Champion for Britain, in classic pose – looking back in triumph over the other three. The moves are unlimited with this game

make the team itself or, if the team is already in the British League (the first division of speedway as it were) you may find yourself loaned to a national league side for a season or two.

If you do become a speedway rider, the amount you can earn varies enormously. Apart from earning money at each event for the number of race starts and scoring points on a three, two and one basis for each first, second and third place achieved, the better riders also receive cash inducements from their clubs at the beginning of each season by way of retainers. There are plenty of financial deals possible through outside sponsors too, from local motorcycle firms to

national brands, either through the supply of discount, free equipment or product endorsement money.

Then by riding on the Continent on free nights – usually Sundays, as British team speedway is held on the other six nights in the season – really large amounts of starting and prize money can be earned, £1,000 being possible for a night's work. The organizers can afford this at European meetings due to the 30–40,000-strong gates they attract, admittance charges in the region of £5 being commonplace compared to Britain's £1.

At the less successful end of the riding scale, £100 per week is common – but bear in mind that the necessary equipment will need some £30 a week to maintain! At the very top, of course, upwards of £30,000 a year can be earned by the star riders.

Most competitors tend to build up their speedway bikes from bits or obtain them second-hand, rather than buy them new, and, being so very specialized, they are certainly far from cheap these days. A good frame will cost about £250; the cycle parts, such as the handlebars, twist-grip, chains and silencer will cost another £200 on top. A front wheel costs £35, a back one £50, the tyres being £8 and £14 respectively. The rear wheel will need renewing, even with turning round between meetings, after every second meeting; the front wheel needs to be changed only four times a season.

Tuning the engine – whether a Jawa from Czechoslovakia or, more usually in recent seasons, a British Weslake – will cost another £650. Then you will need a special set of cams at £150; a high-performance ignition set-up at £100; on the transmission side, a countershaft (really a one-ratio gearbox) at £40; and the competition clutch at £100. You will also need some sort of vehicle to transport the bike to and from the meetings.

Apart for the bike itself, a competitor's budget will also need to cater for the specialist clothing that a rider requires. A good quality, multi-coloured, individually tailored, all-leather riding suit can cost £100 or more. Do not skimp on a helmet. Buy the best you can possibly afford, even though they can cost up to £65 or more. There are the specialist boots too, at £30 a pair; the left one requiring a steel strap-on slipper sole, costing another £10. Goggles, of course, should be top quality ones, and a pair of really strong gloves will be needed, with padded backs to protect your hands from being damaged by flying shale, another £20 or so.

When you arrive at a meeting – and you should be there at least an hour beforehand, not at the last minute – do not waste any time at all by chatting to other competitors or the fans. Walk round the course to see conditions for yourself. You need as much advance notice as possible of the sort of grip the shale is going to afford you. In fact, the top riders will have two bikes with them, one geared for slick, dry conditions, and the other one for deep, grippy conditions, the sort of ratios required for dry or wet conditions being quite different.

You should make the most of the official warming-up period, making sure that you have no problems with your engine, and that it will start and run cleanly. When you are allowed out onto the track for a race, and required to ride up to the starting tape, edge the bike as close to the tapes as possible without actually touching them. Do not rev your engine up until you see the green 'under starter's orders' light come on. When it does, rev the engine up to make sure that you have plenty of motor to withstand dropping the clutch. Then, from the moment the green light comes on, you should concentrate on nothing else but the tape in front of you.

When you make a racing start in speedway, do not spare the clutch, drop it out as quickly as you possibly can, with one sudden action. Unlike circuit racing, you should not try to feed the clutch in at all. Release the clutch suddenly and let the back wheel spin, with the engine working away in the power band from the start.

From then on in the race, grip your handlebars and remember that there is only one control – and that is the throttle. You steer the bike with your back wheel and not the handlebars, something which newcomers often fail to realize. The more revs you can achieve at the back wheel, the more the bike will turn to the left; the less throttle, then you turn to the right. All your corners should be left-handers of course!

Another thing novices always seem to get wrong is that they place too much importance on the left leg. The right leg in speedway is far more important, for it has to take your weight, particularly when you lift your body's weight out of the saddle as you approach a corner to move yourself forward over the front of the bike. You should only use the left leg for a split second to help you turn the bike – and then only in the first instance.

I am often asked about how one should cope with accidents – and they can happen in speedway just as they can in any other form of motorcycle sport. But there is no standard procedure. If you do have time to react at all during a fall, try to avoid making your body rigid. This is easier said than done, I know. But if you do, you are less likely to hurt yourself . . . and you should not contemplate speedway riding unless you are prepared for this. Even the stars fall off sometimes.

9 Rallying

Road Rallies

The least complicated type of motorcycle sport is 'rallying'. Here is sporting motorcycling which even the provisional licence holder can do, for a rally 'seventies-style does not necessarily require any competitive riding nor any large amount of specialist expertise. Motorcycle rallying these days can be simply an excuse for a get-together with fellow enthusiasts.

It can involve members of one or more motorcycle clubs, and often owners of one marque or several designated marques. All the competitors converge on a predetermined rally venue, which might be as basic as a field with a beer tent, attracting about 100 riders, or as elaborate as Britain's number one in the motorcycle rally scene, the Dragon Rally in North Wales, which has become so popular that they have to limit the total attendance to 1,500. On the Continent, the grand-daddy of all rallies, the Elephant Rally, held in the Eifel Mountains, recently attracted in excess of 30,000 two-wheel fans, and its unwieldy popularity is such that the organizers are hastily looking for a less accessible meeting place!

Apart from the fun of travelling to and from a rally, the larger gatherings have the inevitable souvenir rally badges for all who reach the official meeting place, and there are usually all manner of prizes to be won too. These can vary from Concours d'Elegance awards for the best turned out machine, often in different classes and for bikes of different ages, to the longest distance travelled to the rally award, according to the home address of the rider. There can also be a trophy for the best 'turn out' by a club, judged in respect of the number attending from an individual motorcycle club.

A rally is therefore a pleasant excuse to meet with fellow motorcycle enthusiasts with little cost involved apart from the petrol, the beer and a token site-entrance fee. The equipment required can be as elaborate as you have ways in which to store it, or as spartan as the number of pockets in your riding suit dictates. Some seem to delight in bringing along enough camping gear to last a long summer – rather than just enough for the overnight or weekend under canvas; others prefer to pack little more than the riding clothes that they stand up in.

Sadly, the more competitive sorts of motorcycle 'road rallying' have become few and far between, ever since the Department of Transport set up the mandatory authorization fees, and the very strict set of rules that now govern the staging of any sporting event which involves motoring on the public highway. However,

Rallying: a gregarious
cross between a jolly
good party and a scout
jamboree, but with
everybody arriving on
motorcycles

Merely to arrive and
collect that souvenir
badge is really reward
enough

there are still some small road rallies held, quite competitive ones at that, which require competitors to visit a series of manned checkpoints, approaching them and departing from them in given directions, while trying to keep to a time schedule.

The most important road rally is the ACU's annual National Rally, a 600-mile 24-hour ride, culminating in a convergence venue such as Dodington Park in the West Country. Riders have to set out from their own homes and, without breaking the speed limits of the land, have to try to visit as many of a set of manned checkpoints as the various control points' opening and closing times permit, yet without exceeding the 600-mile maximum nor arriving at the finish point after a certain time. The most efficiently planned and executed piece of route selection and execution, as well as the putting up of good performances on special tests at the finish venue, will determine the prize-winners.

Ever-increasing petrol costs have not helped the road rally cause. However, several of the classic road trials still survive, such as the Motor Cycling Club's trio of evergreen annuals: the Land's End, the Exeter and the Edinburgh Trials. These involve all-night runs followed by timed schedules over a series of off-road 'special sections', usually in the form of infamous hill-climb sections, most of which are used every year on these events.

In the case of the Land's End, several starting points are used, something which used to happen in the bad old days on all such events, when simply motoring anywhere tended to be an adventure, let alone storming a series of steep, uphill byways to try to reach the top without falling off or having to seek assistance.

However, be warned, the sections on such surviving classic trials can invariably be very hard on the machinery. Obviously, good maps, sound machine preparation, a good selection of spares, a comprehensive tool kit, and thoroughly warm and waterproof clothing are all needed to tackle this particular brand of challenge. And as far as the less serious and more social 'rallies' are concerned, to find out when and where these are being held, as well as to whom you need to apply to take part, you should scan the announcements in the two major motorcycling weeklies.

The Police Method

Whether you are riding to and from a rally or merely going to work by bike, the vulnerability factor of motorcycling is ever present. Therefore even the most competent enthusiast can usefully benefit from some of the riding methods pursued by the most experienced working motorcyclists of all – the police motorcycle riders.

The correct handling of a motorcycle calls for a variety of mental and physical skills on the part of the rider, and by applying thinking techniques, a high degree of effienciency can be achieved, a system in which a rider and his machine combine to form a relaxed but totally controlled team. To provide a basis on which these good riding techniques can be built, the police have devised their own system for safe motorcycle control. It is designed as a drill, to be put into practice whenever a rider is approaching any hazard or set of circumstances which will require an alternative of speed or course.

Each feature of the police rider's system should be taken in sequence as follows:

1 *Course selected* Look behind, directly or in the mirror – and give a deviation

signal if necessary. Place the machine in its correct position for negotiating the hazard, signalling your intention before you do so.

2 *Rear observation, signals and brakes* Before braking, look behind again and give a slow-down or deviation signal, or both if necessary. Use your indicators (if fitted). This is to inform other traffic of your intention and to ensure a safe speed of approach to the hazard.

3 *Gear* If necessary, change gear to match your speed.

4 *Rear observation and signal* Look behind again – before considering a further deviation signal to inform following and approaching traffic of your intentions.

5 *Horn* If necessary, to warn others of your approach (they may not have seen you or could be out of your view).

6 *Rear observation* The lifesaver, this one. Always take a last look behind you, before you commence your turn, to make sure that following traffic has reacted correctly to your signals.

7 *Acceleration* To leave the hazard safely, taking into account road surface and traffic conditions. There are three types of acceleration which may be applied as soon as the machine is travelling on a straight course again after a corner: (*a*) delicate – where the camber is adverse or where the surface is loose, greasy, highly polished, or covered with leaves; (*b*) normal – used when the machine is again travelling on a straight course, on a good road surface; (*c*) firm – used to accelerate rapidly on a straight course out of a danger zone.

The police rider's ten commandments of motorcycling are also certainly worth bearing in mind:

1 *Know the Highway Code by heart and practise it* The Highway Code is the road user's bible. Observing the Code will make our roads safer and more pleasant for everyone. The Code contains rules for the guidance of all road users. Ride to the Highway Code and you will ride safely and well.

2 *Concentrate at all times and you will avoid accidents* Concentration is the key to good driving. Total concentration will ensure that no detail is missed which might indicate a possible hazard – and will thereby avoid an accident. Concentration also improves machine control. Concentration assists anticipation.

3 *Think before acting* It is a fallacy to think a good rider rides automatically. It may appear so, but every bend, corner or other hazard is a problem overcome by concentration and thought. It becomes an art to ride well, carrying out every operation or manoeuvre in plenty of time. Think ahead – and avoid accidents.

4 *Exercise restraint – hold back when necessary* By exercising restraint and keeping your distance from vehicles you intend to overtake, you will not only ensure your own safety but avoid annoying other drivers by cutting in too quickly. A good rule to remember – whenever in doubt, hold back.

5 *Ride with deliberation – overtake as quickly as possible* Good riding calls for quick and accurate decisions which should be executed with deliberation. Overtaking must be carried out in a minimum of time, so that the road is left clear for opposing or overtaking traffic. Think positively – act with deliberation. Deliberation eliminates uncertainty.

6 *Use speed intelligently – ride fast only in the right places* A speed limit does not necessarily mean that it is safe to ride at that speed – it may, in fact, be dangerous

Riding interesting roads, talking bikes with fellow enthusiasts, this is what the majority of motorcycle rallies are all about these days – relatively cheap and non-competitive

110

in certain traffic conditions. At 60 mph a motorcycle travels 88 feet in one second! At least a second elapses between seeing an emergency and actual application of the brakes. Any fool can ride fast enough to be dangerous.

7 *Develop your motorcycle sense and reduce wear and tear to a minimum* Machine sympathy reduces wear and tear. It also adds to your safety by ensuring that you are in the right gear at the right time. Good motorcycle sense increases the life of your machine too.

8 *Use the horn thoughtfully; if no signals, use your lights* Aggressive use of the horn is as bad as insufficient use. Use the signals as shown in the Highway Code. Use your dipped headlights at night, even on well-lit roads. Give good signals – earn the praise of other road users.

9 *Be sure your motorcycle is roadworthy – know its capabilities* Regular checks will prevent the use of a defective machine. On a strange machine, be familiar with its capabilities and controls before riding fast. Motorcycle and rider must work to ensure good riding.

10 *Your roadcraft – acknowledge the courtesies of other road users* Good roadcraft not only prevents accidents but makes riding less tiring. Set an example to other road users, be courteous and acknowledge their courtesies to you. Courtesy is a great factor in road safety.

In addition, some of the police riding hints are useful too:

Protective clothing You should choose your gear so that it is not only weatherproof but will provide you with the best possible protection against impact and abrasion in an accident. For sooner or later even the best rider can become involved in an accident.

The most important item of clothing is your helmet. Generally, the more you pay for one, the better its quality and so the protection that it is likely to give you. A full-face helmet keeps you out of the weather the best. But in wet conditions, or at night, the conventional open-face helmet allows the use of glass-lensed goggles, which provide better visibility at such times than the integral helmet's plastic visor.

Leather gloves are best. They will not only be warmer, but will give you much the best protection in an incident, being less likely than gloves made from synthetic material to be rubbed through by the road surface. Gloves should always be worn too, however hot or wet the weather, for the day you forget to put them on could well be the day that you fall off – and need them!

Although you can wear rubber boots, leather ones are preferable, even if they do cost much more and require more maintenance. They also provide a great deal more protection to you, because they have sturdier soles and provide you with better support for your ankles.

Real leathers are better than plastic riding suits. But once again, they cost very much more and also require a waterproof oversuit when it rains. They need to be treated regularly with leather soap if they are going to remain in a reasonable state over the years. Leathers should also be as colourful as possible so that you are conspicuous on the road. So wear the brightest suit you can, or make sure you wear a fluorescent over-jacket. Sadly the statistics indicate that most accidents involving motorcyclists are usually caused by the motorist failing to see the unfortunate rider. Remember, a rider and motorcycle have only one quarter of the frontal area of a car. So, even in the daytime, making yourself as conspicuous as possible must be a very wise precaution – presumably, a good enough reason to ride during the day with your headlight on.

The right machine Apart from the prime consideration of whether or not you can afford to run the machine even if you can meet the payments, you should buy a motorcycle that fits you. So often, particularly with some of the superbikes that one sees on the roads these days, it seems too few riders do.

Market leaders, Honda, give some useful advice to their customers on the subject. They recommend that you must be sure that you can sit comfortably astride the machine with both feet on the ground; be able to wheel it along and manoeuvre it in circles without undue effort; and be able to pull it onto the centre stand easily.

On the road, a proper riding posture is the basis for safe motorcycling. Before mounting your machine, set it up on its centre stand and get on. Then stand straight up on the footrests. Keep your toes pointed straight forward. Raise your arms over your head. Then sit down, lightly gripping the fuel tank with your knees. Bring your arms down, placing your hands on the handlebars. Relax your shoulders and arms. Now move the handlebars to the left and to the right – and if your shoulders do not move to the horizontal plane, then you are sitting in the correct riding posture.

Other tips from Honda are certainly worth passing on too. Your eyes: do not look constantly in one direction, but divide your attention fairly evenly over a wide area. Your shoulders: keep them as naturally relaxed and loose as possible. Your elbows: keep them lightly inward and relaxed. Your hands: grasp the grip centres on the handlebars in such a way that you squeeze the grips between your thumbs and index fingers, never holding them too loosely. Your knees: lightly grip the fuel tank at all times. Your feet: keep them pointing straight forward, with the arches firmly placed on the footrests.

Thinking distance This is the distance travelled between the moment the riders sees the need for action and the moment he takes that action. This will vary in accordance with the speed of the machine, the mental and physical condition of the rider, and the degree of concentration given to his riding.

Concentration This requires the full application of mind over body to a particular endeavour, to the complete exclusion of anything not relevant to that endeavour. Concentration imparts the ability to vary the speed of the machine according to existing road and traffic conditions when braking is not demanded.

Principles of cornering – position, speed, gear Cornering requires correct positioning of the machine on the approach, the correct choice of speed, and the correct gear for that speed. These three principles will ensure that the machine will always be on the near side of the road, able to remain there, and capable of being stopped in the distance the rider can see to be clear.

Rules of braking Brake only when straight and upright. Always brake in plenty of time. Brake pressures should vary according to road surface conditions. So firm braking is needed for coarse, dry roads and gentle braking for loose or slippery surfaces. Always watch the road surface ahead very carefully indeed.

On long, steep descents, brake firmly on the straight sections. Only use the rear brakes on the bends, and take a low gear at the start of any descent. Avoid using the front brake when the machine is banked over, turning, whenever traversing wet cambered surfaces, or where the surface is slippery, loose, greasy, icy, polished or leaf covered. The golden rules of braking in safety are: on good road surfaces, braking should be 75 per cent front brake and 25 per cent rear. On good wet surfaces, this should be 50 per cent front, 50 per cent rear – both evenly distributed.

The police motorcyclist's method can perhaps best be summed up by stating that a motorcycle should always be in the right place, travelling at the right speed and with the right gear engaged. Observe this sage dictum and ride on in safety.

10 Machine Preparation

Bike Maintenance

As with any type of sport where mechanical equipment is involved, maintenance – and preventative maintenance – is essential. For having the machinery in as near perfect order as possible is the only way you stand any chance of being competitive. It also pays to keep continually on top of the pre-event preparation, thus avoiding being faced with having to replace everything all at once, rather a daunting prospect at today's prices.

Whatever branch of the sport you enter, it is virtually essential to know every nut and bolt on your machine. You should try to collect the right size spanners around you, ring spanners preferably, although perhaps a comprehensive socket set is best of all. Then apart from the usual essentials, such as a hammer, screwdrivers (both Standard and Phillips – of various sizes, as appropriate), a faithful Mole-wrench and the inevitable rolls of tape and wire, a torque wrench is essential, especially when it comes to securing nuts and bolts which tighten up onto alloy components.

Keep some Loctite handy for treating any threads that are subject to the effects of vibration. Whenever a component is really crucial, you should consider drilling and wiring the components involved. In the case of circuit racing, it is now mandatory to have oil drain plugs drilled and wired, so that they cannot shake loose around the circuit and let all the oil drop onto the track.

The first thing you need to do between rides, whether the machine is for motocross, trials or merely going for jaunts along green lanes, is to keep the bike as clean as possible. Always wash off mud when it is wet; you will find it so much easier to shift than when it has dried on like cement. Be careful you do not use too high a pressure of water or you could swamp the electrics and force water inside the carburettor. Apart from making subsequent re-starting difficult, you might cause water to enter right down inside the cylinders – on a two-stroke, and this could cause internal engine damage.

Collect together a set of suitable cleaning brushes to help you clear away mud from all the bike's nooks and crannies. Loosen the really stubborn mud with a brush; a stiff-bristled paint brush or a washing-up brush can be most effective, particularly for cleaning between the spokes and for removing mud from the springs at the back. Do not be afraid to use plenty of water to soften the mud as much as you can, for there will be less likelihood then of your scratching the machine's brightwork. If you have towed your bike anywhere and therefore have a support vehicle in attendance, make sure you take along plentiful supplies of water to make cleaning the bike as easy as possible.

Having removed all the mud, start your motor up; warming it up certainly helps to dry out any water that may be lurking around. If however you intend to ride the bike immediately, remember that the brakes may be full of water, and therefore need to be dried out gently.

If the machine is a two-stroke one, and the majority of competition off-road bikes still are these days, the maintenance process is relatively uncomplicated and can be easily mastered even by a youngster, once it has been initially explained by an adult mechanic. Even the more sophisticated off-road engine can be dismantled completely in a very few minutes. For motocross one needs to dismantle the engine right down to its basic components for a detailed examination every dozen or so meetings. Four-stroke machines are more complicated, and one needs expert advice on their maintenance.

The best way for any rider to really get to know a machine is, quite simply, to take it to bits and put it back together again. The best way to find out how to do this is to start off with a wholly second-hand machine which needs one or two things putting right. Do not be afraid to ask the experts, particularly a local motorcycle dealer – after all, you have to buy your spare parts somewhere.

From the very start of competition bike ownership, ensure that you always use the correct sized spanners and screwdrivers for the nuts, bolts and screws involved. If you try to save time by using the first tool that comes to hand, it will only make the long-suffering nut, flats or screwhead even more difficult to undo or do up the next time. So, gather together the right tools for the various jobs that you will have to do around the motorcycle.

The first and most frequent maintenance task on an off-road machine is looking after the chain. Whenever any rough ground has to be traversed and taken at a reasonable speed, the chain comes in for rather a hard time. If you have just washed the bike down, use an old rag to clean off any globules of water and mud that may have been left behind after your hosing, then carry out a thorough (and regular) inspection, link by link. If all is well, be sure to relubricate it before you ride anywhere. By far the easiest way to do this is to employ one of the aerosol chain lubricants. Hold up a rag behind the chain when you apply the spray, so that you do not plaster the rest of the motorcycle with chain lubricant. You should try to get into the habit of lubricating your chain every time you take the bike out.

Even with regular spray lubricating, you should periodically remove the chain altogether to eliminate the build up of mud, grit and grease, cleaning it thoroughly by bathing it in paraffin overnight – and boiling it in a large tin of proper chain grease, which, as you might imagine, is potentially an extremely messy business and one that is rarely likely to win you many friends in the kitchen!

However boring it may seem, regular and total removal of the chain for cleaning and relubrication must be undergone. If you continually coat the chain with grease *in situ*, you will only be trapping in more and more dirt, thus reducing the flexibility of the links, and so its life, and invariably causing it to 'lubricate' the rider during the race with greasy missiles!

You will need to adjust the chain regularly. If you have a genuine trail or motocross machine, you must allow for what could be considerable suspension movement, so do not be tempted to over-tighten the chain, even though it may well sound quieter, particularly on the overrun, to take out the slack. With the bike static and the chain not under tension, ideally there should be about two inches of play on the chain's longest run. Do not worry if the chain trails over one of the frame's tubes on the overrun. This can be annoyingly noisy – but, surprisingly for a competition bike, in practice it does not matter.

If you do adjust the chain too tightly and indulge in some low flying, the chain can tighten up and even snap after a solid landing. On the other hand, if the chain is too slack it will be flailing about and will tend to wear out very quickly indeed. If you are in any doubt about your particular bike's chain installation, consult your dealer. Generally, two inches of play on your longest run is what will be required.

Naturally, if a fair mileage on the rough is enjoyed, then the air filter will need regular attention too. Particularly in hot weather it is amazing how quickly the filter becomes clogged up with flecks of earth, deceased flies and bits of grass. If you go in for a motocross event, and especially if it is really dusty, you should consider cleaning the air filter in between races, either replacing its paper element or blowing the dust out of the element (if it is a 'dry' type).

In wet weather it is the air filter which prevents the inlet of water and mud from upsetting the engine's internal activities. If a paper air filter element is used, as long as it is still dry, it can be employed again, once a local garage's air line has eliminated the dirt. However, if it is at all wet, a new element should be fitted. The same de-dusting process can be used on sponge-rubber elements, as long as the element is dry. However, if the rubber is wet, it can simply be washed through in soapy water and dried thoroughly before replacing.

There are those who also believe that, having cleaned the air filter housing and element, they should also coat the intake throat into the carburettor with a thin film of grease, in order to catch any dust or foreign bodies that might find their way through the filter. There is also the highly practical modification available for many machines of a plastic cap to fit over the carburettor body, to keep mud and muck away from the carburettor as well as to make water ingress more difficult.

Even with keen attention to the air filter, the engine oil of a four-stroke should be changed far more regularly than would be the case on a road bike. For, apart from the greater likelihood of a lubricant becoming contaminated through dirt mixing with it, trail bikes will usually be equipped with much lower overall gearing then most road bikes – and so 'off road' engines are certainly likely to have to work very much harder on the way to and from the rough stuff.

Indeed, whatever type of off-road riding you go in for, dirt seems to find its way into everything, the gearbox oil being no exception. In an ideal workshop, this should be drained and renewed at the same time as the engine oil for a four-stroke machine, and at least every thousand miles for a two-stroke. Particularly in high summer, if you are riding a four-stroke motor hard, regular oil changes are essential if you want to keep your engine wear rate down. The oil in the primary chain case should also be renewed for every meeting. Remember to check that the forks still contain an adequate amount of damping oil. The keen enthusiast will also remember to drain and refill the front forks periodically with fresh damping oil.

However, since most riders in British events must become accustomed to competing in the rain, the machine should be prepared accordingly. The high tension lead and connectors should occasionally be sprayed with a water-repellent silicone-type aerosol spray, and for fending off the dreaded engine stall, where really large water splashes have to be traversed, the high tension side of the electrics should be completely coated with silicone grease. This may look rather messy, but it could keep you going where others fail.

Another tip is to ensure that the gap between the contact breaker points' hatch and the engine is sealed properly. Use a really substantial strip of adhesive tape, a coating from an aerosol water-repellent spray or, once again, a film of silicone grease. The only thing to remember is that you may possibly be sealing off the means of ventilation and, if it is a really wet day, it may therefore be as well to check occasionally for any build up of condensation within. To do this you will need to remove the points' cover to dry out any water drops that might be there.

Quite obviously, pitted points should be changed just as soon as you spot them, as they can not only upset an engine's starting performance, but also cause a power-reducing misfire. The recommended points' gap should be regularly checked and maintained.

On any two-stroke, the sparking plug will need to be checked and changed far more regularly than is the case with any four-stroke engine. Particularly with motocross work, you should become used to the idea of taking a look at your spark plug between every race. Every time you return to the workshop, you should give the plug a really good clean, checking and readjusting the gap as necessary. Do not be mean with your engine either, and treat it to a new plug just as soon as the electrodes show any signs of wear. It really is false economy to keep struggling on with old plugs. Strangely, many do.

Oil the cables regularly, adjusting them as necessary. To this end, you will quickly discover that experienced riders make a point of actually removing the inner cables from their outer sheaths. They will be looking for the start of any fraying, and will also be lubricating the inner cables along their whole length before reassembly. Several experts seem to prefer using oil for this job rather than grease, presumably finding that there is less likelihood of the cable sticking as a result.

If there is any chance of a cable's outer sheath jumping out of its steering slot, then tape should be stuck over the release concerned; watch for any chafing of any of the outer sheaths. If the outer cover is badly worn through, it should be changed, and the cause of the chafing eliminated. If not, then the outer covering should be cushioned with a few turns of binding tape. So often cable runs are particularly vulnerable where they trail across components, frames competition number plates or handlebars. When adjusting cables, be careful not to overdo the front brake adjustment. Ideally, there should be some free play, or it could snatch and throw you.

The clutch should have some free play too, a quarter of an inch or so makes for an easier clutch operation. You will therefore be operating the clutch nearer to the handlebar, which is far more convenient for most riders. Clutch and brake lever covers are vital for serious off-road motorcycle sport, preventing, as they do, the ingress of both water and grit which can all too easily make the controls sticky —

and can also shorten the life of cable ends. The levers themselves should be screwed on tight enough to the bars to prevent their slipping round. However, if the levers are too tightly secured, they could snap off in a fall. They therefore need to be secured well, yet without being completely solid on the bars. The levers need to be ball ended, they nearly all are these days anyway.

Even with a brand new competition bike, you may need to either change the bars or reduce their width slightly, by taking equal amounts off either side, to suit your own personal preference. The standard ones can very often be either too high or too low. Again adjustment or a change of bars may be needed. Comfort and controllability must come before looks. Certainly many of the so-called instant 'trail bikes', mass produced as they are, are on sale with handlebars that are far too high.

Wherever any rough going is encountered, the footrests come in for a very hard time indeed. However careful a rider you are, the footrests will occasionally be making contact with substantial objects, which, together with the sort of frenzied vibration of which even the smallest two-stroke engines are capable when they are extended, make footrests rather prone to cracking through as a result. It would be extremely dangerous for a footrest to give way when you are standing up on the pegs, and are at that moment totally dependent on them.

You will need to see that your rear wheel is properly lined up in the frame, otherwise the machine will crab along the straights and become less easy to handle in a tight spot. The chain should be carefully lined up between the sprockets, so that it is not pulling sideways at all. The rear sprocket retaining bolts tend to work loose every now and again, so these have to be checked along with all the other nuts and bolts on the machine. Whenever you have the rear wheel clear of the ground, check for excessive sideplay in the rear suspension arms. These pivot joints take plenty of punishment on an off-road bike, and so periodically need re-bushing.

Check the wheels for loose spokes. On off-road work, they tend to loosen off with alarming regularity. Form a habit of tightening your loose ones regularly – but beware of over-tightening them. If you do, you will ruin the wheel rims by pulling them hopelessly out of shape. Anti-creeping bolts round the wheel rims should have their nuts checked periodically for tightness too.

When you have any spare maintenance moments, it is worth removing the wheels altogether from the bike to dismantle the brakes and clean out any brake dust and dirt that may have found its way inside the drums. If there is still adequate meat on the lined shoes, you should take the opportunity of emery-papering the surface of the linings to remove any glazing. The mechanical parts of the brakes should be greased – but only very lightly, as any over-lubrication, particularly when the brakes become hot, could cause the grease to run and so contaminate the brake linings. On reassembly, ensure that the brake actuating arms are free-moving.

Obviously any grease nipples, such as those on cables, should be regularly greased. The steering head bearing will need greasing too – and occasional adjustment if it is either too tight or too loose. If you ignore this, the ball-bearings within can become damaged.

The oil level in the forks, as already mentioned, should be regularly maintained, while the spring-damper mountings at the back should be given frequent checks for tightness. The dampers should, of course, be changed if they become soggy.

Rough going and dust also do their worst to the wheel hub bearings, which need to be dismantled occasionally and greased. To do this, you will need to remove the wheels from the frame. Attention to the bearings – by greasing them occasionally – can make them last for a surprisingly long time. Another 'economy' measure is occasionally to change the rear tyre round so that the other sides of the tread come into use.

If the fuel tank springs the slightest leak, or is in any way suspect after the bike has been dropped, it is far too dangerous to do anything else but have the tank professionally repaired or, expensive though it may be, fit a new one.

Quite obviously, if you do ride your machine in the most extraordinary places, you will need to keep a careful watch on the tyre walls, being sure to investigate any cuts in them as well as any possible inner tube movement. During any type of sporting riding, your tyre pressures should not be forgotten either. Both the competition bike sales specialists and the tyre manufacturers should be able to give you a recommendation as to the best tyre pressure to use for your particular bike and type of motorcycling.

There really is nothing in the basic maintenance with which straightforward common sense and an average set of tools cannot cope. After a while, even opening up an engine, particularly if it is a two-stroke, should not be too difficult for most enthusiasts. The majority of off-road sporting motorcycles are fitted with perfectly straightforward and entirely logical single-cylinder two-stroke units.

The first internal check for such an engine is to check the condition of the cylinder's bore. The pistons should be examined too – as well as the rings – to ensure that satisfactory compression is possible. Then both the small and big ends need to be checked for excessive free-play and renewed if necessary. The most frequent task will be to de-carbonize the head, piston top and ports, while after dismantling any engine for an internal inspection it is wise to take the opportunity to renew all the various oil seals and casing gaskets.

Once you have persuaded the engine to go back together again, certainly for the first time, you will probably need to employ the assistance of an experienced mechanic to show you how to check up and adjust the ignition and carburettor properly. It is very elementary, once you know how. Like so many things in the motorcycle world, the tricks of the trade in machine preparation and maintenance can be picked up, entirely for free, by keeping your eyes and ears open both in the paddock car park and in the bar afterwards.

Race Preparation

Keeping the machine clean is one of the basic prerequisites of competition motorcycling; it is especially prudent for circuit racing of course, where the speeds are likely to be much higher. The very act of cleaning the engine and motorcycle parts periodically helps to unearth actual or potential trouble spots. This checking should obviously be a fairly constant activity too, and ideally any maintenance work should be of a preventative nature rather than merely renewing a component once it has failed, for then it could be too late.

Start with the front end of the bike – the front wheel in particular. Remove this from the frame, so that you can examine it more closely and conveniently on the workbench. Like many of the jobs on a bike, you only need to carry them out once a season or, if a particularly heavy season is contemplated, between each batch of races.

Deflating the tyre thoroughly, release the tyre securing bolts, if fitted, and, employing tyre levers in the usual way, peel the outer cover and inner tube from the rims for a thorough inspection. The tyre should have plenty of tread on it, and not a trace of damage. The tube should be free from patches, because, at high temperature and under the considerable stresses generated from racing cornering speeds, such repair places must make the tube potentially weaker. A new inner tube is cheap enough after all. In any case, changing a repaired tube for a new one

Price tags, as with anything mechanical, can be unlimited – at £3,500, they do not come much more expensive than this 750 MV poem in alloy

should only be necessary if you have bought the bike second-hand.

If a drum brake is fitted to the wheel, carry out an internal examination by dismantling the brake and the wheel bearing. Clean out old brake lining dust, check the state of the linings, replacing them if there is any likelihood of one of the rivet heads reaching the surface of the lining, and so possibly scoring the braking surface of the drum. If the linings used are bonded to their brake shoes, and there is any chance during a race of the linings wearing down and the metal of the shoes making contact with the drum, then quite obviously the lined shoes should be changed.

A badly scored drum surface should be reground, or, if very deeply marked, replaced altogether with a new drum. Clean out any old grease that may have escaped from the wheel bearing, and any grease that has found its way onto the brake shoes; then the linings should be changed for new ones.

When repacking the old wheel bearing again with new grease, or fitting a new bearing, be sure to use only very high melting point grease because, under racing conditions, the necessary braking can generate colossal temperatures, and you do not want grease to melt within the brakes.

Disc brakes are now far more likely to be used for both brakes; they are much simpler, and the necessary visual checks can be made externally in no time at all. Check that the disc is securely attached to the wheel and, if it is scored, have it reground or replaced with a new one. Check the caliper for fluid leaks, and overhaul it if necessary, using new hydraulic seals. As for dangerously worn brake pads: they can be instantly spotted on disc brakes and should be changed for new ones (preferably ready bedded-in from the practice seassion and marked as to which side of the caliper they belong) – so that they will be instantly at home when action commences. In fact, with linings or pads, if there is any doubt about how long they may last, the workshop is the place to change them. If any movement at the wheel spindle is detected, then replace the spindle and bearing components. Do the wheels both run true? As a general rule, a spoked wheel (rapidly being replaced in most classes of circuit racing with an alloy wheel) should have a maximum of only an $\frac{1}{8}$ inch play. With a wire wheel, none of the spokes should be loose at all. Before you replace the tube and tyre, check that none of the spoke ends are over-sharp, as you do not want them chafing through the inner tube later on.

Once a tyre has been replaced onto its rim, check the balance of the wheel and rectify it, if necessary, by adding weight to the appropriate spokes. Check the front forks for controlled movement as well as for any excessive play in the steering head races, and the bushes too. Also ascertain whether the oil seals are doing their job properly and there is still oil in the forks to damp the springing adequately. You do not want over-tight steering head bearings; if their movement is found to be rough, they are either dry of grease or one of the ball-bearings has a high spot.

The rear wheel should be checked for sideways play when it has been refitted to the frame, since this might indicate either excessive play in the rear wheel bearings or badly worn suspension arm pivot bearings – or even that the spindle itself has become too badly worn to be used again.

The rear damper/spring units should be changed if they have gone soft. However, unless you really know how to set up a bike, do not be tempted to experiment with softer or harder springs or shock absorbers, it is much wiser to follow the

Compact and potent, Suzuki square-four, disc-valve 500, nestles innocently in its owner's frame – ready with 90 bhp at 10,500 rpm. In top, that means 174 mph

ready-developed advice of riders who have been riding similar mounts for some time.

As with off-road bikes, do not try to skimp on the cables. If any doubt about their condition exists, change them. Do this anyway if you consider that the inner cables have been in use for some time. The last thing you want is a cable to part – or even stick – when you are racing. If a new cable, inner, outer, or both, has to be fitted, do this before the practice, so that the initial stretching of the cable can be taken up by adjustment before the extreme operations of the race itself.

Ensure that all the various controls, front brake and clutch levers, rear brake and gearchange pedals, as well as footrests and handlebars, all fall readily to hand and foot respectively. The optimum slipstreaming crouch may be achieved by repositioning or adjusting the bars and/or the footrests. But is there sufficient ground clearance for the corners? And can you still change the gears smoothly, without hunting for them?

Fairing nuts, bolts and screws have a great deal of stress to contend with, even on the smoothest-running multis. Very frequent checks should be made for their tightness. Always use washers under screw or bolt heads as well as washers and spring-washers for the nuts, which should ideally be of the Nyloc variety, the threads wisely being treated with Loctite before tightening.

11 Clothing

Apart from the safety aspect, you need to dress for motorcycle sport so that you ride comfortably as well. The right clothes must necessarily be something of a compromise, but you should choose clothes carefully so that you are neither too hot nor too cold, and certainly so that none of your vital movements are at all restricted. Rules on clothing vary from one type of motorcycle sport to another, as stated in the various regulations, particularly in terms of the compulsory crash helmet specification. Apart from the fairly obvious roadgoing gear required for motorcycle rallying and on/off-road green lane work, the types of sporting motor-cycling dress vary according to the principal divisions: trials, motocross, circuit racing, grass track work and speedway.

Trials gear
Surprisingly, for many years crash helmets were not considered essential wear by trials riders – even by the top trials stars who had to negotiate some of the nastiest and most rock-strewn terrain one could possibly find. They preferred the old cloth cap instead! Today, however, particularly if any part of an event includes some motoring on public roads, link sections between the observed ones, wearing a crash helmet is compulsory by law.

For trials work you should select a helmet which is as light as possible but which allows you to hear as much as possible, too. Most full-face, integral helmets are not practical on both counts. You obviously want the minimum strain on your neck muscles. This is where the advisability of wearing a light helmet comes in. You may also want to be able to spin your head round suddenly in the middle of a section, to reappraise the next part of the section. A heavy helmet will hinder you in this, as will the deep-sea diver aperture of an integral one. You will also want to hear what your engine is doing at anytime, so you can make it do something entirely different within a split second.

Most of the top riders wear an open-face helmet offering temple and side of head protection, but one which sports a detachable peak. The peak is most useful for fending off the odd clod of earth that might be thrown up by the front wheel splashing into a boggy puddle. Goggles are rarely necessary, unless the weather is incredibly bad or the event is a long one, such as an international six-day trial. A visor is simply impractical; it gets in the way and can become scratched far too easily. A peak is also useful to keeping the sun out of your eyes; wearing sun-glasses is not to be advised on safety grounds because they break far too easily.

The well-dressed motocross man enters battle

125

Besides, you want the maximum amount of visibility when it comes to peering your way through a shadowy part of a section which may pass under some trees.

Proper leather or rubber trials boots – and not just any old roadgoing motor-cycling boots – are essential. Rubber boots are far more practical than leather, and they are much cheaper too. Cleaning is relatively simple. Whatever their muddy state, you can merely kick them off at the end of a trial and wash them down along with the motorcycle. However, do not think gumboots will be suitable; you need the industrial-type rubber boots, which are fitted with steel toecaps for safety. On the other hand, although they are far more expensive, leather boots do give you more support and allow you a greater feel of the pedals and footrests. Cleaning them at the end of the day however is fairly time-consuming. Whatever type of boots you choose, you should wear a pair of thick-knit 'fisherman's' socks inside.

Any beginner should equip himself with a pair of gloves. What you lose in sensitivity with the controls, you gain in protection for the knuckles if you fall off. As most British trials are held in the winter's worst, your hands are far more likely to be warmer with gloves than without. Losing feeling in the fingers makes for very difficult handling of the controls. Even in hot conditions, keep wearing those gloves.

The most expensive item of personal equipment is likely to be a trials suit. Again, do not try to use any old items of clothing, even clothing that is specifically for motorcycling. A trials suit is made for the job, and a great deal of development work has gone on behind the scenes to get the product right.

Even though more and more riders seem to have been opting for the cheaper, one-piece nylon or cotton oversuit in recent years, the best all-round choice, particularly when one considers having to contend with British weather, is one of the traditional Barbour suits (marketed under such reputable brands as Belstaff). These old-style trials suits are just as waterproof, much warmer, have more pockets usually, and invariably include more useful padding for when you fall off, than the more recent ranges. However, a nylon suit is very much easier to clean after-wards.

Whatever type of suit you choose, wear some warm and practical clothing beneath if it is a cold day. Buy a size that is comfortably big enough, as you do not want to be constricted in your movements. Do not choose one that is too outsize and loose, or it will flap about and get in the way. Wear the overall trousers outside the boots so that, on a really soaking day, water does not fill them up!

What the 'Best Dressed Motocross Rider' should be wearing

For motocross, an ACU approved helmet must be worn, one carrying the official ACU transfer of approval. This means that the helmet must be BSI 1869, 2495, 2001 VU, SHCA (Safety Helmet Council of America) or Z90 (another American standard). Chincaps (following the controversy of their being worn by riders on the road) are not permitted on the primary fastening of a helmet. If the helmet that you purchase does not carry the ACU stamp, then it can be submitted to the ACU's headquarters with a fee of 30p (plus 70p, at the time of writing, to cover the cost of return post and packing) for them to check your helmet over, and pass and stamp it accordingly. It is naturally preferable to select a helmet which has already been accepted by the ACU and which therefore carries their stamp ex-factory.

126

In addition, the ACU insist on 'protective clothing' being worn, consisting of breeches, gloves, knee-length leather boots, and long-sleeved jerseys, again only those carrying the ACU stamp, or garments which are likely to offer similar protection. Goggles and spectacles, if they need to be worn, have to be of a non-splinterable material.

The equipment listed above represents only the basic clothing you should consider. You should be prepared to change certain items almost on an annual basis, particularly your helmet, which after a full season will tend to become shabby and ineffective. Even if it looks as if it is in reasonable enough condition, do not economize, change it. It is your head, after all. Helmet straps tend to become less effective with age, and the performance of the main material of the helmet's shell does deteriorate with time, whether it be polycarbonate or glassfibre.

The ideal helmet for the motocross rider is much the same as that used by the trials man – an open-faced one with a peak, preferably a 'duck-bill' extended one, which is particularly effective in fending off large clods of earth flung up by the rear wheel of the rider in front. Do not be tempted to paint up an old helmet to rejuvenate it. If the surface looks tired, then it will be less efficient, and the whole helmet should be changed. The potential problem with painting a helmet is that you may cause a chemical reaction to take place between the paint and the helmet material which actually weakens the shell. The rule always holds good that the more expensive the helmet, the better it is likely to be.

The second most expensive item of kit is a pair of motocross boots. Buy good quality ones, preferably those which have padded fronts and sides as well as slipper soles rather than separate heels, so that the sole is integral with the heel. The soles of your boots should be able to skate over rough ground when you are steadying yourself or pivoting the bike round on your leg. Steel reinforcement for the toe, instep and heel helps to make them last longer. Synthetic materials surprisingly seem to be just as hardwearing as traditional leather over a full season.

Leather trousers are essential. Usually, the more you spend, the longer they will last. Buy proper jeans that are specifically made for motorcross riding out of really strong cowhide, and which have padded knees and a padded seat as well.

Good quality gloves must be worn to prevent palm blistering, and ward off potential damage to the fingers from flying missiles. Avoid gloves that have seams which could rasp on your hands and form blisters; many do. There is now quite a range on the market in the motocross glove line. Certainly avoid a thin pair; choose instead those which have padded palms.

To complete your action wardrobe, you will also need: a pair of plastic-lensed goggles; a face mask, preferably a plastic one which clips from one side of the helmet to the other, so protecting the jaw and the whole of the lower part of the face; an anti-vibration bodybelt, which is quite essential; a set of chest and shoulder armour shields, which, although they feel a little strange to wear at first, are a wise investment when it comes to protection during a fall; a full-sleeved and sturdy motocross shirt, as required by the regulations; and a waterproof but light-weight oversuit, essential for riding on watery events.

Circuit racer haute couture
Whether circuit or road racing, the ACU insist that the rider wears a crash helmet

with their 'approved' stamp. Leathers are mandatory, as are leather gloves and leather boots, no gaps being permitted between the boots and the leather coverings for the legs. However, sidecar passengers are allowed to opt for light-weight footwear instead, and most choose baseball boots. All participants must wear goggles or visors, made of non-splinterable material. In addition, identification discs are required for racing, to be worn round the neck or wrist. These should show your full name, birth date and blood group.

Apart from your machine, the scrutineer will also want to check your clothing to see that it complies with the regulations and is in a reasonable condition. It is false economy to try to save money by using items of clothing that are obviously second-rate. If they become damaged in a spill, then suspect leathers, boots or

Racing haute couture – in leather. Hahne, BMW's star, in the Bol D'Or

gloves should be repaired before you race in them again. A battered helmet shell or frayed attachment strap definitely calls for instant replacement, as do scratched goggles or, in particular, visors, which seem to last no time at all unless great care is taken of them inbetween meetings.

As integral helmets have increasingly taken over for racing in recent years from the open-face version, face masks are less common. But if you do decide on an open-face helmet, a mask is essential, and, for safety in a fall, it should preferably be a leather one. In the absence of a mask, a handkerchief worn across the face bandit-fashion will do for a mask, and is certainly better than nothing at all.

A weatherproof, if not waterproof, oversuit is essential for bad-weather riding. However, ensure that you use a suit that fits you properly; one that billows about will significantly affect your aerodynamic performance and so your top speed.

Look after your leathers. If they become wet, do not artificially accelerate their drying as this will only harden them, and lead to premature cracking. They should be cleaned only with a proper leather soap, and should also occasionally be treated with a leather preservative of some kind to make them more comfortable to wear and more waterproof.

Oval world gear

The ACU helmet rules for circuit racing apply to speedway riders too. However, the full-face integral helmet is rarely worn; riders prefer the open-face variety instead. Peaks are essential, and the regulations demand that these are detachable and are made of a flexible material.

If racing in dry conditions, goggles must be worn, and they must be made of non-splinterable material. For wet weather racing a visor is to be preferred, ideally a hand-operated swing-up swing-down one, which can be operated in a split second – possibly in the middle of a corner. In the wet, shale can be flung up from the rear wheel of a rider in front, and can form a fairly effective method of grit-blasting, so the face also needs to be protected by a face mask, preferably a leather one, in addition to a quickly operable visor.

Even though the speedway rider is rarely likely to be out in the open for more than three minutes at a time and actually in action for little more than 60 to 70 seconds, a really well-made one-piece set of racing leathers is vital. Indeed the sport's regulations demand that these are not only made of leather but are substantially padded at the shoulders, elbows, hips and knees. In addition, riders will usually be required to wear over-vests, carrying their team's symbol on the front and their own competition number on the back. To make identification even easier for the crowd, competitors are also asked to wear one of four 'colours' – red or blue if they belong to the home team, and white or yellow and black if they are with the away team. This is usually achieved by riders wearing elasticated coloured helmet covers. If the weather is extremely bad, then obviously competitors all wear nylon, wet-weather oversuits over their leathers.

Speedway regulations also insist on riders wearing knee-length boots, and again leather ones are the standard equipment. For the left 'sliding' foot, competitors need to strap on a skid to the bottom of the boot, which is really a steel slipper, starting with a toe cap and going back under the whole length of the sole. Leather gloves are mandatory too, preferably ones that are well padded on the outside to protect

Oval wear for the world of team speedway

the fingers from being abrased in a tumble.

The same conditions and requirements apply to the equally 'oval world' of grass track racing too, where both riders and, in sidecar events, their passengers will need to be similarly attired.

12 Transporting the Motorcycle

Such is the sheer competitiveness of even club level motorcycle sport these days that it is generally considered impractical to ride the motorcycle on the road to and from events, except in the most local of trials where the journey on the road is quite short. Riding trials tyres for great distances over tarmac destroys their edges, while the low overall gearing of the trials bike makes heavy going of any realistic cruising speed. There is always the risk, too, that the bike will break down on the trial, and the rider will be left with no means of return transport.

Some years ago, one of the most popular ways to transport a competition motorcycle to and from events was, rather oddly, in the cradle of a sidecar frame, the rider driving the complete sidecar outfit to and from the venue. Today the ways of taking a machine to a meeting are various in the extreme – in cars, on the back of cars, on bike trailers, in vans, or in those highly suitable (but hard to find) pick-ups. Your choice of transport, of course, depends on your budget as well as the sort of season you may have in mind. But whatever method you eventually choose, you will be wise at first to spend some time at one or two meetings to observe what systems other competitors have adopted and, indeed, what tips you can learn from their mistakes.

Car brackets

There will be few motorcycles small enough, and few cars big enough, for the bike to be carried inside the car – or, for that matter, inside its boot. The most usual method is for a bracket to be fitted to the back of the car, and this is the transporting system followed by most speedway competitors. They attach a U-channel section strip of steel to the topside of a proper towing bracket, and run up a pair of anchoring stays from this for the bike to lean against and to be attached by straps. Avoid fitting any bracketry directly onto the car, as this is rarely likely to be satisfactory, particularly when it comes to trying to sell it.

Try to space the bracket (and the machine) away from the rear panel of the car. You may find it necessary to remove the front wheel of the bike to reduce the overall length of the machine, thus preventing either end of it from sticking out past the sides of the transporter vehicle. One snag with this transporting arrangement is that access to the rear of the vehicle, especially the boot, is likely to be restricted. You may have to unload the machine from its carrying bracket before you can extract anything from the boot.

Car and trailer

Perhaps the most convenient way of transporting a competition motorcycle is by the ordinary road car and trailer. The rider then has a completely unspoiled means of family and commuting transport, which can double up, by merely attaching the trailer, to become a competition transporter. The most popular hitch for the rear of any tow bracket (and you must fit a properly engineered one) is a 50 mm ball coupling. Most people fit this size as it is interchangeable with nearly every other car that can be converted for towing on the road – a useful point, if your own car should ever break down at any time and you need to borrow a friend's car to tow you to an event. However there is always the danger of theft; the risk of having your trailer and competition bike speedily towed away by a complete stranger is certainly a grave one.

If you have to leave your trailer outside your home, use a non-standard pin and eyelet towing connection, for which burglars are hardly likely to be equipped for an instant tow job. You can also fit the pin with a sturdy lock-pin. Certainly any tow car and trailer should be fitted with a safety chain, just in case the trailer should break adrift, and your valuable cargo be scattered all over the motorway.

The law on trailer lighting is very strict, so do not skimp on trailer lights – a DIY lighting installation rarely seems to work for long. It is far better to obtain a proper and professionally manufactured trailer lighting board, as the various lights and reflectors are made to legal specifications and the board is ready wired to a really sturdy cable. It will also be already fitted up with a multi-pin plug of the correct type to fit the multi-pin socket, which you should have had fitted to your tow car's bracket. In many cases, it may not be practical to mount such a trailer lighting board permanently. Indeed, it may hamper the speedy removal of the bike when you arrive at the venue. So try to evolve some reliable fixing arrangements which will allow the board to be attached to and removed from the trailer as necessary.

The law requires that a trailer lighting board must be fitted above 1 foot 3 inches and below 3 feet 6 inches from the ground. Remember to take along some spare light bulbs; as it does not matter how well suspended a trailer is, the bulb life tends to be fairly short. Although many competitors do run with solid suspension trailers, both the trailer and the bike will suffer much less if the trailer is equipped with adequate suspension; the best system is a pair of suspension torsion arms, proper trailer units set in rubber, or at least coil or leaf springs.

Until you are well practised, reversing a trailer can be far from easy. With a two-wheeled trailer, there is a 50 mph maximum speed limit in Britain. When loading your bike onto the trailer, weight distribution needs to be carefully planned, and the height of the tow hitch on the car's towing bracket may need adjusting accordingly. Whether you are towing motorcycles or anything else, you need to tell your insurance company – and be sure that the contents of the trailer are themselves insured. After all, accidents can happen, even to the best prepared outfits.

Unfortunately, even a simple design of motorcycle light-weight trailer can be very expensive to buy ready-made. Once upon a time, a bike trailer could be picked up, even brand new, for £30 or £40. Today, prices are much higher, and, not unnaturally, it has become financially attractive to many to consider construct-

ing their own trailer. It really is not all that difficult. All you have to do is to make an accurate copy of any professionally-made bike trailer you may see at a meeting.

The extent of the construction depends on the workshop facilities to which you have access. If you do not possess cutting equipment of sufficient strength, you can usually obtain the necessary steel lengths, ready-cut to the measurements required. Use mild-steel angle iron for the main runs, as this is not too brittle if you weld it together, the angle giving the trailer strength without needing the weight of box-sectioning. If you have no welding equipment, you can just as easily drill and bolt your trailer framework together, although it is more time-absorbing. If any joint is of doubtful strength, add gusseting braces across the corners.

To carry one bike, you will need a single channel attached to the middle of the trailer. If you want to take more than one machine, then you will need to organize further channels on either side of the trailer to balance up your outfit. Use U-section steel strip for the bike runner, over-ordering so that you have a further strip left over to use as a bike ramp. This can be either hinged to the runner or slotted in place where necessary and carried in the tow car's boot when not being used.

Having wire-brushed all loose rust off your fabrication, spend some time rust priming the trailer with zinc paint and finishing it off with several coats of a good tough black paint. You should also paint the underside with an underbody protective paint, particularly if it must stand outside the house in all weathers. Rubber mudguards are by far the best choice for the trailer wheels as they do not suffer from corrosion. If you have the time, box in the trailer's girders; it not only makes a much neater job, but it can also help to ward off much of the road dirt from the bike. It also prevents you from dropping a wheel through the trailer's framework when you are loading and unloading.

The front end of each bike runner needs to be fitted with a sturdy 'stop' to prevent the motorcycle from running into the back of the tow vehicle. This is also required for fastening the bike, since it is preferable to use a proper safety belt and buckled straps, rather than an old length of rope. The safety belt will be less prone to fraying, will be easier to clean and, once wet, will not tighten up through shrinking. I use four such buckle straps, fastening the bike down at each corner. You may need to introduce eyelets into the trailer's construction to assist you in this.

Finally, do not forget to take along a spare wheel as well as a suitable jack and the right wheelbrace for the trailer wheel nuts. This is rarely remembered. One problem with a trailer is that a motorcycle – even with an adequately secured Sammy Miller motorcycle cover – does become well covered with road filth and, on a wet day, really mucky spray. Indeed, after a long run on a bad day, the polished parts of a bike can actually become damaged, being almost grit-blasted by small stones on the road.

Vans and pick-ups

Undoubtedly a van has all the advantages for carrying your motorcycles and attendant equipment around. A van will supply you with room to take along all the various tins of fuel and lubricant, the vital toolbox and spares – even a spare bike, if you like. It also supplies you with a really useful place to work on your machine if the weather turns bad. And if you want to save on the hotel bills, then the van can offer overnight accommodation too.

If a van is for you, then ideally choose one where the storage area is separated from the cab section, thus affording you far better insulation from road noise when you are on the move. Take time to prepare the inside of the van, so that there is a place for everything and everything can be in its place. You can do a great deal of damage to your equipment – not to mention your bike – if the contents are allowed to slide around all over the place. Build storage racks and clips to securely fasten everything down.

As the loading area of a van is likely to be a fairly long way off the ground, you will certainly need a ramp system to facilitate the loading of the bike itself. A tent extension is not a bad idea too, since it provides extra room in the dry to store things when you require the maximum amount of working space inside the van.

One way to run a van economically is to share the costs with other competitors, since it is possible to accommodate several bikes in a medium-sized van. Beware of buying a 'bargain' van second-hand, for unlike cars, people rarely part with vans if they are in reasonable condition. Even the most conscientious transport manager will want to extract the last penny from his commercial vehicles before parting with them. As a result, most second- or third-hand vans on the market are likely to be in a poor condition. So a really thorough overhaul will be essential before the necessary reliability can be hoped for. You need to prepare your means of bike transport just as efficiently as you do the competition machine itself. Sadly, it seems, few competitors do. A needless breakdown on the way to a meeting is just a complete waste of time.

A big advantage with a van, particularly when the route involves motorways, is that you do not have to worry about speed limits as you do with a two-wheeled trailer. Also you can use the cheapest two-star petrol, or diesel fuel if the van has a diesel engine, so that your fuel costs will be appreciably lower over a season than would be the case with a petrol-engined car.

Large estate cars can be usefully employed for bike transport, although their tailgates usually render access through the hatchback rather high up, thus requiring a ramp, and the height of the aperture itself is often a problem if the machine has high-rise handlebars.

Perhaps the best answer to the problem of transport is the pick-up. As with a van, it means that only one vehicle has to be paid for when it comes to cross-Channel ferry bills. It is more manoeuvrable than a van, and certainly much more nimble than a car and trailer, and again is not restricted to the same speed limits as a car and trailer, always a factor to consider on really long hauls to and from meetings.

Whatever form of transport you choose, it is a sensible precaution to make out a check-list of all the things your particular branch of the sport requires, so that nothing is left behind – as can so often happen during the usual late Friday night scramble before you set forth for a long haul to some meeting at the other end of the country.

Do try to be totally self-sufficient as far as your catering arrangements are concerned. It does not seem to matter which part of the country you are in, the standard of British paddock catering is almost universally inadequate. Besides, taking your own food along will save you money – and that will always come in useful in emergencies.

List of Addresses

The booming two-wheeled world is teeming with entrepreneurs and specialists for every conceivable aspect of sporting motorcycling. But owing to the rapid rate of commercial growth, the movement of the personnel involved and the changes of address are a constant and bewildering process. Apologies are therefore made in advance for any errors resulting in the following list from subsequent expansion and take-overs, and for any omissions of the newcomers. The reader must obviously check first by telephoning the firms concerned before travelling.

Motorcycle Specialists

Air filters
UNI-KE FILTER PRODUCTS, The Shipyard, 42 Island Wall, Whitstable, Kent CT5 1EW (Whitstable 63952)

Brakes
Competition brakes
PAGEHILN LTD, Railway Works, Elmham, Dereham, Norfolk (Elmham 631)

Competition lining materials
FERODO LTD, Chapel-en-le-Frith, nr Stockport, Cheshire SK12 6JP (Chapel-en-le-Frith 2520)

Relining shoes and pad supplies
BETA BRAKES, 16 Lower Bond Street, Hinckley, Leicestershire (Hinckley 30859)

Cables
REDFEARNS SOUTHAMPTON, 37 Northam Road, Southampton SO9 4LQ (Southampton 26634)
VENHILL ENGINEERING LTD, 6–8 Lincoln Road, Dorking, Surrey (Dorking 5111)
V & M MOTORCYCLES, Greenfields, Kerry, Newton, Powys SY16 4LH (0686-88596)

Camshafts
LINKS ENGINE DEVELOPMENT AND RACING, 10 School Lane, Baston, nr Peterborough (Greatford 440)

Carburettors
AMAL CARBURETTORS LTD, Holford Road, Witton, Birmingham B6 7ES (021-356-4801)
DELLORTO CONCESSIONAIRES, Boult Street, Reading, Berkshire (Reading 598955)

Chains
DID CHAINS, H & S Motorcycle Parts and Accessories, Unit 14, Bordon Trading Estate, Oak Hanger Lane, Bordon, Hampshire (Bordon 3555)

Competition Motorcycles and Specialists
BULTACO motocross and trial, as well as KTM motocross and enduro
COMERFORDS LTD, Oxford House, Portsmouth Road, Thames Ditton, Surrey KT7 0XQ (01-398-5531)

CCM motocross (four-stroke specialists)
CLEWS COMPETITION MACHINES, 48A Shifnall Street, Bolton, Lancashire (Bolton 22720)

Chassis kits and customizing
RICKMAN BROTHERS (ENGINEERING) LTD, Stem Lane, New Milton, Hampshire (New Milton 613838)

Customizer
DRESDA AUTOS LTD, 292 Worton Road, Isleworth, Middlesex TW7 6EZ (01-568-4753)

All eyes – including the Section Marshal's – on Bill Wilkinson. No need to bother. He cleaned it OK

CZ motocross and trail, as well as Jawa ISDT motocycles
SKODA (GB) LTD, Bergen Way, North Lynn Industrial Estate, Kings Lynn, Norfolk PE30 1BR (01-253-7441)

Four-stroke engine preparers
S & S PERFORMANCE LTD, Unit 6, The Maltins, Roydon Road, Stanstead Abbotts, Hertfordshire (Ware 870899)

HARRIER enduro
AJW MOTORCYCLES LTD, Andover, Hampshire SP10 3LU (Andover 51155)

HUSQVANA
BRIAN LEASK (MOTORCYCLES), County Oak, Crawley, Sussex (Crawley 25037)

MAICO motocross
BRYAN GOSS MOTORCYCLES LTD, 9/10 Westbury, Bradford Abbas, Sherborne, Dorset DT9 6SQ (Sherborne 27897)

OSSA motocross, enduro and trial
OSSA MOTO (UK) LTD, Ferndown Industrial Estate, Ferndown, Dorset (Ferndown 71449)

MONTESA trials, motocross and enduro
JIM SANDIFORD (IMPORTS) LTD, 30–38 Walmersley Road, Bury, Lancashire (Bury 8204)

Production motorcycle conversion equipment
DIXON RACING LTD, Farncombe Street, Farncombe, Godalming, Surrey GU7 3BA (Godalming 21010)

Production engine conversion equipment
PIPER FM LTD, Wootton Road, Kings North, Ashford, Kent (Ashford 24681)

Racing everything
BARTON MOTORS (CAERNARFON) LTD, 31 Castle Square, Caernarfon, North Wales (Caernarfon 3944)
COLIN SEELEY INTERNATIONAL, Old Forge Works, Stapley Road, Belvedere, Kent (38-46006)
TERRY SHEPHERD, Old Vicarage Farm, Southport Road, Scarisbrick, Lancashire (Scarisbrick 74454)

Schoolboy scrambler and trial
YAMOTO (MOTORCYCLES) LTD, Hickstead, Bolney, Surrey (Crawley 34505)

SUZUKI motocross, trial and schoolboy scrambler
BEAMISH (MOTORS) LTD, 121–123 Gardner Road, Portslade, Sussex (0273-592953)

Trial and enduro, parts and preparation
SAMMY MILLER EQUIPMENT, New Milton, Hampshire (New Milton 616446)

Cylinder Heads

Compression raised
RUSKIN ENGINEERING, Tingley Mill, Bridge Street, Morley, Yorkshire (Morley 536309)

Electronic Ignition
LUCAS ELECTRICAL COMPANY LTD, Great King Street, Birmingham B19 28F (021-554-5252)

Electrical Repairs
CHAPMANS, South Queens Branch, Dock No. 1, Liverpool L3 4AJ (051-708-0797)

Magnetos and dynamos
DAVE LINDSLEY, Buckley Mill Garage, Oakenbottom Road, Bolton, Lancashire (Bolton 34104)

Electronic ignition and rev counters
P.E. ROBERTS, 2 Lancing Road, Woolton, Liverpool L25 9QB

Forks

Supplier of Betor forks
RICKMAN BROS, Stem Lane, New Milton, Hampshire (New Milton 613838)

Repairs
WILKES ENGINEERING LTD, Meeting Lane, Brierley Hill, West Midlands (0384-75596)

Frames

Repairs
WILKES ENGINEERING LTD (address as above)

Goggles and Visors
MELTON SAFETY PRODUCTS LTD, 102–104 Church Road, Teddington, Middlesex (01-977-4635)

Heavy Duty and Competition Shock Absorbers
J.W.E. BANKS & SONS LTD, Crowland, Peterborough PE6 0JT (Crowland 316)
GIRLING (Parts and Service Division), Birmingham Road, West Bromwich, West Midlands B71 4JP (021-553-2969)

Girling repairs and service
EXPRESS AUTO SERVICES LTD, Crown Road, Twickenham, Middlesex TW1 3EU (01-892-5421/2)

Helmets

Bell
SHANE HEARTY MOTORCYCLE CLOTHING, 96 Beckenham Lane, Bromley, Kent (01-464-4700)

Centurion
THETFORD MOULDED PRODUCTS LTD, Mill Lane, Thetford, Norfolk IP24 3DA (Thetford 4266)

Cromwell
ROY OF HORNCHURCH (ENTERPRISES) LTD, 35 High Street, Hornchurch, Essex (49-42323 and 56289)

Griffin
GORDON SPICE LTD, 12 Central Trading Estate, Staines, Middlesex (Staines 50221)

Kangol
KANGOL HELMETS, 3 Commerce Road, Stranraer DG9 7DF (Stranraer 3631)

Nolan
KEN COBBING LTD, Munro Industrial Estate, Waltham Cross, Hertfordshire (Waltham Cross 24981)

Owen
CHARLES OWEN AND COMPANY (BOW) LTD, 82/102 Hanbury Street, London E15 (01-247-2488)

Paddy Hopkirk, Agordo and Jet
MILL ACCESSORY GROUP LTD, 2 Counties Mill, Eaton Bray, Bedfordshire (Eaton Bray 220671)

Read
PHIL READ, The Thatched House, Oxshott, Surrey

Stadium
QUEENSWAY, Enfield, Middlesex (01-804-4343)

Most makes
JOHN BROWN WHEELS (various branches, details from Head Office), Wedgnock Lane, Warwick, Warwickshire (Warwick 46131)

Helicoiling
ALF SNELL ENGINEERING, 126 Boundary Road, London E17 (01-520-5222)
GARD AUTO ENGINEERING SERVICES, Rayleigh, Essex (Rayleigh 747410)
OVERHILL MOTORCYCLES LTD, 140 Lowfield Street, Dartford, Kent (Dartford 20781)
REG CHILD, Geoffrey Street, Preston, Lancashire (0772-588144)
RUSKIN ENGINEERING, Tingley Mill, Bridge Street, Morley, Yorkshire (Morley 536309)

Leathers
INTERSTATE LEATHERS, 70 Wellington Road, Northampton, Northamptonshire (Northampton 31760)
KETT MANUFACTURING COMPANY LTD, 10/16 Byron Road, Wealdstone, Harrow, Middlesex HA3 7TA (01-427-7767/8/9)
D. LEWIS LTD, 124 Great Portland Street, London W1 (01-636-4314)
GEOFF DARYN MOTORCYCLES, Strand Street, Sandwich, Kent CT13 9KP (Sandwich 2161/3901)

RIVETTS LTD, 234/8 High Road, Leytonstone, London E11 (01-334-3021/1304); 143 Grosvenor Road, London SW1
TT LEATHER INTERNATIONAL LTD, 56 Montalbo Road, Barnard Castle, Co. Durham (Barnard Castle 2191/3495)
G. WADDINGTON & SON LTD, Newland, Hull HU15 2DL (Hull 443101)

Repairs for all leathers
SUEDE AND LEATHER CARE, 30 Preston Street, Brighton BN1 2HP (Brighton 27488)

Lubricants
BEL-RAY LUBRICANTS, Involute Works, 17b Middlemore Lane West, Aldridge, Walsall, Staffordshire (Aldridge 51155)
CASTROL LTD, Burmah House, Piper's Way, Swindon, Wiltshire (Swindon 30151)
DUCKHAMS OILS, Summit House, Glebe Way, West Wickham, Kent (01-777-0600)

Magneto Servicing
JACK COOPER RACING MAGNETO SERVICE, 5 South Street, London SE10 (01-858-2239)
DAVID LINDSLEY, Elton Vale Works, Elton Vale Road, Bury, Lancashire (Bury 4105)

Major manufacturers of road-going motorcycles
Batavus and Moto Morini – HARGLO LTD, 462 Station Road, Dorridge, Solihull, West Midlands (Knowle 5835)
Benelli and Garelli – AGRATI SALES (UK) LTD, 76 Marks Street, Nottingham NG3 1DA (Nottingham 50616)
BMW CONCESSIONAIRES (GB) LTD, 991 Great West Road, Brentford, Middlesex TW8 9ED (01-568-9155)
Casal – ALAN TAYLOR (NORTHERN) LTD, Elm House, Manchester Road, Castleton, Rochdale, Lancashire (Rochdale 33221)
COSSACK UK, Satra House, 359/361 Euston Road, London NW1 (01-387-2866)
DERBI CONCESSIONAIRES LTD, Bremar House, 27 Sale Place, London W2 1PT (01-262-2271)
DUCATI & MOTO GUZZI CONCESSIONAIRES LTD, 19/25 Crawley Road, Luton, Bedfordshire (Luton 26903)
Fantic – BARRON EUROTRADE LTD, Fantic House, High Street, Hornchurch, Essex (Hornchurch 58158)
Gilera – DOUGLAS (SALES AND SERVICE) LTD, 1/2 Oak Lane, Fishponds Trading Estate, Bristol BS5 7XB (Bristol 654197)
Harley Davidson – AMF INTERNATIONAL, 25 Old Burlington Street, London W1X 2BA (01-734-8070)
HONDA (UK) LTD – also trail of course– Power Road, Chiswick, London W4 (01-995-9381)

KAWASAKI MOTORS (U.K.) LTD – also motocross and trials – Radix House, Central Trading Estate, Staines, Middlesex TW18 4XA (Staines 51444)
Laverda – SLATER BROS, Collington, nr Bromyard, Herefordshire (Kyre 294/5)
MOBYLETTE MOTOR IMPORTS COMPANY LTD, 700 Purley Way, Croydon, Surrey (01-681-3911)
NVT MOTORCYCLES LTD, Lynn Lane, Shenstone, Lichfield, Warwickshire (Lichfield 480633)
STEYR-DAIMLER-PUCH (GB) LTD, 211 Lower Parliament Street, Nottingham NG7 2DD (Nottingham 56521)
SUZUKI (GB) LTD, 87 Beddington Lane, Croydon, Surrey (01-689-8111)

Nuts and Bolts

Also sockets, screws, taps, dies, drills and 'Allen' screws
CDS SCREWS, Grove Road, Northfleet, Kent

Off-Road Clothing
BELSTAFF INTERNATIONAL LTD, Caroline Street, Longton, Stoke-on-Trent (Stoke-on-Trent 317261)
JOHNSONS AND SONS LTD, North Quay, Great Yarmouth (Great Yarmouth 50311)

Everything for the trials and motocross rider
SAMMY MILLER EQUIPMENT, Gore Road, New Milton, Hampshire (New Milton 616446)

Racing Numbers
STAGE THREE PRODUCTS, David Ison Ltd, 50/54 Charlotte Street, London W1 (01-636-3541)

Reboring Specialists
LEN LEVENSON, 219 Wood Street, Walthamstow, London E17 (01-520-1087)

Ring Seating and Port De-burring Equipment for Two-Strokes

Flex-Hone
NITRO (LEAMINGTON) LTD, Frome Hall Mill, Lodgemore Lane, Stroud, Gloucestershire (Stroud 5867)

Shot and Bead-blasting
CARLOW ENGINEERING, Manor Trading Estate, Benfleet, Essex (South Benfleet 55122)
DRESDA MOTORS, 292 Worton Road, Isleworth, Middlesex TW7 6EL (01-568-4753)
KENDON ENGINEERING COMPANY, Leaventhorpe Lane, Bradford BD8 0EG (Bradford 881616)
KILBOURN MOTORCYCLES, Mead Lane, Chertsey, Surrey (Chertsey 63321)

MORPHY MOTORS, Tring Road, Long Marston, nr Tring, Hertfordshire HP23 4QL (0296-668030)
REDDITCH SHOT BLASTING, Heming Road, Washford Estate, Redditch, Worcestershire (Redditch 29659)
SOUTHERN BLAST CLEANERS, Western Road, Shoreham, Sussex (Shoreham 2800)
WILKES ENGINEERING LTD, Meeting Lane, Brierley Hill, West Midlands (Brierley Hill 75596)

Spares Sources
MCA (ASTON) LTD, 40/50 Victoria Road, Aston, Birmingham B6 5HF (021-554-6644/3011)

Sparking Plugs
CHAMPION SPARKING PLUG COMPANY LTD, Great South West Road, Feltham, Middlesex TW14 0PH (01-759-6442)
NGK SPARK PLUGS (UK) LTD, 24 Burnt Mill, Elizabeth Way, Harlow, Essex CM20 2JW (Harlow 418321)

Speedway and Grass Track
DV GODDEN ENGINEERING, Blacklands, Mill Street, East Malling, Maidstone, Kent ME19 6DR (0732-844072)
ALF HAGON PRODUCTS LTD, 350/352 High Road, Leyton, London E10 6QQ (01-539-8416 and 01-556-9200)

Spokes
LEMET METAL WORKS LTD, George Street, Birmingham B3 1QE (021-236-6676)

Sprockets
PAGEHILN COMPANY LTD, Railway Works, Elmham, Dereham, Norfolk (Elmham 631)
SUPERSPROX, Roger Maughfling Engineering, Station Works, Knucklas, Knighton, Powys (Knighton 201)

Stove Enamelling
CHUNAL MOTORCYCLES, 13 Charlestown, Glossop, Derbyshire (Glossop 61864)
DRESDA AUTOS, 292 Worton Road, Isleworth, Middlesex TW7 6E2 (01-568-4753)
HOUGHTON FINISHES (STOVE ENAMELLERS), Unit 3, Howard Road, Redditch, Worcestershire (Redditch 25945)
RAYMOND ELLIS (DECORATIONS) LTD, Central Street, Hull, North Humberside (Hull 27737)
S & B SCOOTERS, 217 Streatham Road, Mitcham, Surrey (01-648-2900)

Tanks

Alloy tanks manufactured
NEWTON EQUIPMENT, 122 London Road, Brentwood, Essex (Brentwood 210530)

Metal tanks repaired and resprayed
BYKE INN, 199 Church Road, Leyton, London
E10 (01-556-0196)
DOBBS & JENKINS MOTORS LTD, Perseverance
Coachworks, Huddersfield Road, Mirfield,
Yorkshire (Mirfield 494644)

Metal and alloy repairs and respraying
MUIRASPEED, 123 Eastern Avenue, Ilford,
Essex (01-550-2237)

Trailers
BUFFALO MOTORCYCLE TRAILERS, Calmar
Trailer and Engineering Co., Totman Close, Weir
Industrial Estate, Rayleigh, Essex
(Rayleigh 73600)

Transistorized Ignition
BOYER-BRANSDEN ELECTRONICS, 38 London
Road, Bromley, Kent BR1 3QR (01-460-1515)
JOSEPH LUCAS (SALES AND SERVICE) LTD,
Great Hampton Street, Birmingham B18 6AU
(021-236-5050)

Tyres
AVON TYRES LTD, Bradford-on-Avon,
Wiltshire (Bradford-on-Avon 3911)
CONTINENTAL TYRE AND RUBBER COMPANY
LTD, Ullswater Crescent, Coulsdon, Surrey
CR3 2HR (01-668-2372)
DUNLOP LTD, Fort Dunlop, Erdington,
Birmingham B24 9QT (021-373-2121)
MICHELIN TYRE COMPANY LTD, 81 Fulham
Road, London SW3 6RD (01-589-1460)

Welding Sets
Gas and arc welding and brazing sets
MARNEY & JACKSON LTD, Northern Electro
Engineers, Whittle Street Works, Tottington
Road, Bury, Lancashire (061-764-7658)

Welding undertaken
WILKES ENGINEERING LTD, Station Drive,
Brierley Hill, West Midlands (0384-75596)

Wheel Building
CENTRAL WHEEL COMPANY, Lichfield Road,
Water Orton, Birmingham B46 (021-747-5175)
RON COMPTON, 109 Brownhill Road, London
SE6 (01-697-2779)
ESSEX WHEELS (DEREK YORKE), 2 Brewers
Yard, Springfield Road, Chelmsford, Essex
(Chelmsford 54358)
HACKING & KAY, Mile End Row, Blackburn,
Lancashire (Blackburn 53204)
ALF HAGON PRODUCTS LTD, 350/2 High
Road, Leyton, London E10 (01-539-8416/
556-9200)
MOTOR WHEEL SERVICES, 71 Jeddo Road,
London W12 9ED (01-743-3532)
J.E. NUNN, 117 Brighton Road, Surbiton,
Surrey (01-399-2455)
RIGHTWHEEL, Bective Road, Putney, London
SW15 (01-874-7708)
WEST LONDON REPAIR CO. LTD, 5 Lancaster
Road, Wimbledon, London SW19 (01-946-6316)

Wheels
Cast alloy
CAMPBRAY & CAMPBELL GEOMETRICS,
Unit D, Burnham Road Trading Estate, Dartford,
Kent (Dartford 22778)

Magnesium alloy
CMA AUTOMOT LTD, Industrial Estate,
Mildenhall, Suffolk (Mildenhall 713700)
PAGEHILN COMPANY LTD, Railway Works,
Elmham, Dereham, Norfolk (Elmham 631)

Work Benches
Grazia Hydraulic
MERTON & WARD LTD, 360 Kingston Road,
Ewell, Surrey KT19 0DU (01-393-2940)

Motorcycling Organizations

BRITAIN

Amateur Motorcycle Association
'Burley'
Sighford Lane
Aston by Poxey
Staffordshire
078-578-476

Auto-Cycle Union
31 Belgrave Square
London SW1X 8QQ
01-235-7636

C.T. Bowring (London) Ltd
(the official brokers of the ACU)
(Competition Department)
Marlowe House
Station Road
Sidcup
Kent DA15 7BW
01-300-7755

Fédération Internationale Motorcycliste
19 Chemin William-Barbey
1292 Chambesy
Geneva
Switzerland
022-58-19-60/1

Motor Cycle Union of Ireland
11 Glen Crescent
Jordanstown
Newtownabbey
Co. Antrim
0231-63564

Scottish Auto-Cycle Union
'Kippilaw'
Longridge Road
Whitburn
West Lothian EH47 0LB
0501-42663

The Speedway Control Board
31 Belgrave Square
London SW1X 8QJ
(01-235-7637)

UNITED STATES

American Federation of Motorcyclists
4996 Argyle Drive
Buena Park, CA 90620

American Motorcycle Association
Box 141
Westerville, OH 43081

Association of American Motorcycle Road Racing
268 East Street
Hebron, CT 06248

Florida Grand Prix Riders
107 Patricia Street
Auburndale, FL 33823

Washington Motorcycle Racing Association
1415 N.E. Iravenna Blvd.
Seattle, WA 98115

Index

ACU (Auto-Cycle Union) 9, 50, 142
ACU Approved Stamp 64, 128
ACU National Rally 109
Adults class 36
Agostini, Giacomo 74
Airfield circuits 64
AMA (American Motorcycle
  Association) 142
AMCA (Amateur Motorcycle
  Association) 50, 142
Apex point 65
Ariel 14, 27
Armco 73
Assen Circuit 75–7
Average speed 42

Baker, Stevie 79
Barbour suit 126
Bashplate 22, 31
BBC Grandstand 52
Bedeldijk 76
Belstaff suit 126
Birch, Ken 83
Birkett, Nigel 13
Bol d'Or 128
Bontoft, Norman 83
Boots 126
Black flag 66
BMW 82, 128
Bowring (London) Ltd, CT 11
Brake pads 122
Brands Hatch 51, 72
Braking point 65
Bridle path 31
British experts 52
BSA 45, 52, 82
BSA Bantam 56
BSPA (British Speedway Promoters
  Association) 101
Bultaco 14, 27, 30, 72

Cables 123
Cadet class 55
Cadwell Park 82
Caliper 122
CCM 45

Cecotto, Johnny 62, 79
Chairs 80
Cheney 45
Chequered flag 67
Chicane 77
Christmas tree 87, 93
Circuit furniture 65
Circuit Paul Ricard 74, 75
Circuit racing 61
Circuit Van Drenthe, Assen 75, 76
Cleaning the section 14, 57
Closed to club 63
Collins, Peter 95, 105
Colours 129
Concours d'Elegance 107
Cotton 19, 20, 45
Courbe de Signes 74
CS Competition Solo 88, 91
CZ 52

Dabs 57
Damper 120
Damping oil 117
Daytona 62
Decibels 71, 94
Department of Transport 107
Desert racer 31
Disc brake 122
Division One 100
Division Two 100
Dodington Park 109
Dot 45, 97
Douglas Twin 102
Dragon Rally 107
Drag racing 87
Drag strip 87
Droylesden 99
Drum brake 122
Duck-Bill Peak 127
Duke, Geoff 74, 78
Dustbin fairing 71, 80, 88
Dutch Grand Prix 75

Eastwood, Vic 48
Edinburgh Trial 109
Elephant Rally 107

Eliminator 87
Enduro racing 29, 38
Epping Forest 99
ESO 102
Exeter 104
Exeter Trial 109
Expert class 58

Fabergé Racing 74
Face Mask 127
Fairing 71
Farleigh Castle 52
FIM (Fédération Internationale
  Motorcycliste) 142
Flange bolts 16
Footing 50
Formula TT 85–6
Full-face helmet 125

Gawley, Jeff 82
Goer 30
Grass track racing 59, 94
Green flag 67
Green lanes 29
Greeves 45, 52

Hackney 104
Hahne 128
Hailwood, Mike 73, 74, 78
Hamel, Yvon du 72
Hawkstone Park 52, 53
Heat leader 100
High melting point grease 122
Hobbs, John 92
Hoge, Heide 77
Homologate 84
Honda 14, 27, 31, 57
Horsfield, Chris 52

Integral helmet 125, 129
Intermediate class 55
International events 63
Ipswich 104
ISDT (International Six-Day Trial)
  27, 31

James   52
JAP (JA Prestwich)   102
Jawa   30, 102, 104, 106
Jumping   47–9
Junior class   55

Kawasaki   72
Kayaba   78
Knievel, Evel   58
Knobbly tyres   33
Konig   83

Lands End   109
Larkstoke   52
Laverda, Jota   32, 61
Leadbitter, Tom   97
L'Epingle   75
Loctite   115, 123
Long Marston   98
Looping the loop   58

Madijk   76
Matchless   45, 52, 53
Mauger, Ivan   95
Methanol   101
Mikuni   78
Miller, Sammy   14, 27, 134
Mistral Straight   74
Mole wrench   115
Montesa   14, 30
Motocross   45
Motocross boots   50, 127
Motocross riding   47
Motorcycle   50
Motorcycle News   50
Motor Cycling Club   109
Motor Cycle Union of Ireland   142
MV Agusta 750   121

National events   63
Nitro   101
Noisemeter   71
Norton   45, 83
Nylon   123

Observed section   13, 45
Oil flag   66
Open-face helmet   125, 129
Ossa   14, 30

Ossebroeken   76
OS (Ordnance Survey)   31, 38
Over-gearing   66
Over-vest   129

Phillips screwdriver   115
Pit signals   52, 70
Pit stops   70
Police Method   109
Production machine class   61
Protective clothing   64
PS (Pro Street)   88, 91
Pure alcohol   101

Racing line   65
Racing school   72
Rallying   107, 111
Rathmell, Malcolm   25
Read, Phil   55, 74
Red flag   66
Restricted competition licence   63
Restricted events   63
Rickman   52
Road racing   61
Roberts, Kenny   62, 79

S (Street)   88
Sand racing   59
Schoolboy scrambling   55
Scott   45
Scottish ACU (Auto-Cycle Union)   142
Scott Trial   45
Scrambling   45
Scrutineering bay   64
Second-hand buying   34
Second string   100
Secretary of the Meeting   50
Section begins – and ends   13
Senior class   55
Service area   42
SHCA (Safety Helmet Council of
   America)   126
Sheene, Barry   55, 71, 74, 78–9
   Short, Gerald   98
Sidecar racing   80–1
Silicone spraying   118
Silver, Len   104
Silverstone   61
Slick tyres   70, 91–2

Slipper-soles   97
Slipstreaming   68
Smart, Paul   71–2
Smith, Jeff   45
Speedway   99
Speedway Control Board   142
Starting   67
Steering head bearings   122
Stekkenwal   76
Split links   43, 51
Stoomdrift   76
Supercharging   88
Surtees, John   74, 78
Suzuki   44, 54, 74–5, 78, 123

Tactical substitute   101
Tear-off lenses   98
Timing beam   93
Time control   42
Timed section   45
Torque wrench   115
Tow, obtaining   67
Trailer lighting   132
Transporting bikes   131
Triumph   89
Tyre pressures   51

Under-gearing   66

Villiers   52, 97
Vincent Black Shadow   82
Virage de l'Ecole   74
Virage de la Sainte-Baume   74
Virage de la Tour   75

Wedge   80
Weslake   102, 106
Wilkinson, Bill   136
Wheel bearing   122
Wheelies   21–2, 58
White City   99
White flag   66
Wire spoked wheel   122

Yamaha   31, 62, 78
Yellow flag   66

Z90, American Helmet Standard   126